The *Dirt* on
Dating

Hayley DiMarco

Revell
a division of Baker Publishing Group
Grand Rapids, Michigan

Hungry Planet

Published by Revell
a division of Baker Publishing Group
P.O. Box 6287, Grand Rapids, MI 49516-6287
www.revellbooks.com

New edition published 2008

ISBN 978-0-8007-3296-7

Printed in the United States of America

The Library of Congress has cataloged the original edition as follows:
DiMarco Hayley.
    The dirt on dating : a dateable book / Hayley DiMarco.
        p.   cm. — (the dirt series)
   ISBN 10: 0-8007-5917-6 (pbk.)
   ISBN 978-0-8007-5917-9 (pbk.)
   Dating (Social customs)—Religious aspects—Christianity—Juvenile
literature. 2. Interpersonal relations in adolescence—Juvenile literature.
I. Title. II. Series.
HQ801.D565 2004
646.7′7—dc22   2004024217

Published in association with Yates & Yates, LLP, Literary Agents, Orange,
California.

copyright

What's inside

The DIRT on DATING

When was your last date? Last night? Last week? Last month? Or too long ago to remember? Maybe you've never had a date at all. Don't worry, that doesn't make you a freak in my book, just a patient person. Sit back and relax, this won't hurt a bit. *The Dirt on Dating* is going to fill you in on the ritual of dating. It's chock full of good stuff about *asking a girl out, calling boys,* and *fresh dating ideas.* It will fill you in on *when to call a guy back, how to let a girl know you're interested,* and a bunch o' other stuff that everybody needs to know about going out with the opposite sex. Whether you have a busy social calendar or you prefer to sit at home and wait for your soul mate to come calling, someday you are gonna need to know how to relate to someone you totally dig.

This book is dating advice with the spirit in mind. Dating isn't just about the physical; there's also the emotional, the moral, the ethical, and the spiritual. How you relate to people of the opposite sex matters. It matters to them, and it matters to God. Unfortunately, the Bible doesn't have anything to say about dating directly, so don't expect to find the final word on the process of dating. What I hope to provide you with is some sort of spiritual compass for how to treat people and how to prepare yourself for marriage, the ultimate goal of dating. Ca-ching!

All of this is to say that what I wanna do is to help keep you from getting hurt but at the same time tell you not to live your life in a closet. Most of this is just good, old-fashioned common sense, but there are a few places where I get to preachin'. Not about dating, 'cuz like I said, the Bible doesn't talk about dating, but about how God asks us to relate to our mates. Again, that's the ultimate goal of dating. If you have never opened a Bible or just choose not to live by any kind of divine law, a lot of this might seem foreign to you, but trust me, there will be stuff in here you can use. This stuff will help you save your heart and the heart of others. And who knows? You might actually nurture your spirit along the way. So sit back, relax, and check out *The Dirt on Dating*.

Bible note

In a couple of spots you will find some Bible study stuff. It might not be what you were looking for when you bought a book on dating. Don't get scared off by all the verses on marriage and all; it's just part of understanding how God sees guys and girls in relationship. I'll try to make it as painless as possible. Without it you'd have no idea where I get my ideas about the roles of guys and girls, so hopefully these verse studies will help.

To Date

To date or not to date—that's the question. Or maybe it isn't. Maybe the real question is, "How the heck do I get a date?" Whatever Q is on your mind, it's *The Dirt on Dating* to the rescue (insert superhero theme music here).

Did you know that dating is a relatively new concept? Yep, in the olden days instead of dating to find a mate, your family would pick one for you. One family met with another family and swapped things to cut a deal. "I'll give you 4 cows for Suzy if you throw in that fine wheelbarrow." Then the lucky couple showed up for the wedding, and the deal was done. It's kinda like some reality TV show where a girl's friends pick her future husband for her and she has to marry him by the end of the season. But times have changed, I guess. At least it has for those of us who don't find the love of our life on national television. We want different stuff now. We have dreams and plans, like college. We wanna see the world. Life just ain't the same as it was back in the day. In Bible times people married because the guy needed someone to cook and clean and the girl needed someone to kill things and protect her. Now we can go to the grocery store for all the food we need and throw dinner in the microwave. Food is not really the reason we get married anymore. Now it's about important stuff like romance, sex, happiness, similar values, and looks. We all want a soul mate. We want a best friend. We want compatibility; we want the dream relationship. And since our demands went from survival to pleasure, we had to figure out a way to find the most excellent partner, and thus dating was invented.

Most people date around till they find the dream, the perfect one, the one that fits, or, in the words of the chick in *Jerry Maguire*, the one that "completes" them. But others wait for the perfect one to come by and then "court" (i.e., date) each other till marriage. Either way, nowadays before we walk down the aisle, we *date* the person. All this to say that unless you are so old-fashioned that you've decided to let your parents choose your mate for you, you've come to the right place. *The Dirt on Dating* isn't about one kind of dating or the kissing off of dating. It doesn't support any particular style of dating like group dates versus one-on-one dates or courting. What it does do is **help you understand the opposite sex** and figure out how to hang with them. So let's get going. Let's find out why in the world you wanna date *now* or why you think you'll just wait till the right one comes along.

If you think that at any point in your life you will date at least 1 person, then read on. *The Dirt on Dating* will help you to better love the person and understand how to relate to them in a godly way. Are you ready for the Dirt? 🐾

Okay, so here's the sitch: when you are in high school and you choose to be a person who dates, you are really choosing to be a person who wants to learn more about themselves and what they want in a mate. (At least that's what I hope. You could just be desperately trying to find someone who will get you out of your parents' house and into your own apartment when you graduate.) But the way I see dating is that it's kind of like a training ground. Dating can be a really good way to figure out who you are and what kind of people you like. Now, maybe you're the kind of person who already knows exactly what they want. You've got it all listed out. Heck, you even know what they are going to look like. Let me just congratulate you on being a psychic. You have a great future reading palms and tea leaves if you know exactly the person you will marry. But most people have no clue. Most of us just have to live and learn. It's like this: It's really easy to say Paris is your favorite city if you've never been there before. But go there and you might end up saying, "Dang, it was better in pictures. In person it's dirty, it's smelly, and the people are just plain rude." Things change over time and with experience.

So dating is kind of like a practice ground for your future. It's the place where you figure out what makes you tick and, more importantly, what kind of person makes you tick. Another bonus of the dating ritual is that when people like you and want to see you a lot, you feel good about yourself. You start to see that your mom wasn't so far off after all when she said you were the best kid in the world. Dating isn't required to make you feel your value, but you'd be crazy to think that it doesn't help. So dating isn't just about marriage. In fact, if you are 15, 16, or 17 years old it isn't about marriage at all. It's just about getting to know yourself and the opposite sex. 'Cuz remember, the crush you have right now will more than likely not be your last, but the impact that it makes on your life will last: 51% of teen marriages end in divorce before the age of 24.*

Okay, if you're still not sure dating is for you, then keep reading. You've got a few things to consider before you plow into something you're unsure of. And if you are totally ready to date or have been dating forever and just want to get on with the good stuff, then keep on reading too. I've got lots of things for you to check yourself on as you walk down the path to dating bliss. ☁

*According to the National Center for Health Statistics.

Lists:

The Good, the Bad, and the Ugly Sides of Dating

Dating has its bonuses and drawbacks. Before I do anything, I like to weigh the pros and cons so I can make a non-stupid decision. Here's the list for you of the goods and the bads of dating. Which make the most sense to you?

Top 5 Dating Bonuses

1 **See what kind of people *like you*.** One of the main reasons you might choose to date in high school is to find out what kind of people like you. The people who crush on you will show you the types of people you will attract as you get older. If you figure out that you are attracting jerks or losers, do some soul searching. Look into what in you is attracting the wrong people.

2 **See what kind of people *you like*.** Just because you think someone is hot doesn't mean you would make a good couple. Dating in high school helps you figure out the types of people you like and see if you really are good together. Do you look for bad guys or naive girls, or are you drawn to healthy people who want a serious relationship? If it's the former, now is a good time to figure out why you like people who aren't going to stick around long. As you start to grow you will find out better ways of attracting good people and avoiding the bad.

As believers we are continually on the road to sanctification, which means being made holy. God is always making us more like Christ and drawing us closer to him. And relationships are a major place where others can see the nasty underbelly of sin that we all still have and also where we can encourage one another and learn more about grace. A dating relationship can be a totally eye opening one because the person you date will bring out things in you that no one else will. If they are faithful, they will share God's love with you like no one else does. If they're not, then you might need to look inside to see why it is that you are drawn to someone who pulls you away from your Savior.

3 **Get to know *yourself*.** Dating is a great way to get to know yourself. As you date you will start to learn tons of stuff about your personality, your strengths as well as your weaknesses. An old proverb says, "As iron sharpens iron, so one man sharpens another" (the ancient book of Proverbs, chapter 27, verse 17). Dating is a great way to smooth out your edges and become more of the person you were meant to be. It's also a great way for you to learn social skills, like how to act when you first meet someone and what to do on a date. It's a relationship training ground for the future.

4 **Figure out your boundaries.** Are you good with boundaries? Or are you a people-pleaser who can never say no? Dating can teach you a lot about protecting the boundaries that are good for you, like not allowing your life to ever be completely absorbed into someone else's. In a healthy dating relationship, you learn how to be your own person while creating an intimate relationship. Having boundaries shows that you care about yourself and who God made you to be.

5 **Learn about the opposite sex.** Face it, they are hard to figure out. But the more time you spend with them, the more you begin to understand them, like how they communicate, how they bond, and what drives them completely nuts, both in a good way and a bad way.

1. **Practicing divorce.** If you date wrong—I mean if you do it in a bad way—then beware, because you could be practicing divorce. When you date, break up, date, break up, and on and on, you can get really good at walking away from someone just because you are tired of them or mad at them. Serial dating, meaning going from one commitment to another, can get you in the habit of practicing divorce. That's why it's so important to understand dating and the opposite sex so that you don't get used to bonding with people you probably won't be with for the rest of your life. Don't allow a life of serial dating to get you comfortable with leaving an unhappy marriage relationship. *"And I say to you: whoever divorces his wife, except for sexual immorality, and marries another, commits adultery"* (Matthew 19:9 ESV).

2. **Sexual promiscuity.** "But among you there must not be even a hint of sexual immorality" (Ephesians 5:3). Face it: date, and things can happen. You have to be totally obsessed with staying pure in order to, well, uh, stay pure. If you get relaxed, dating all the time, being alone with your little hottie, then look out, things can go fast. It's like this: Today, kissing might be all you need with your love, but next week kissing won't be enough and you'll find yourself shirtless. Then, well, you know the progression. I think Giuseppe said it best, "Date and you run the risko of fooling aroundo." Don't date, and you are home free on the fooling around stuff.

3. **Broken hearts.** Everybody, sing it with me, "Love hurts, yeah, yeah, love hurts." Face it, no one can hurt you more than someone you love. It goes with the territory. Love me and you give me all kinds of ammo for hurting you. And chances are, I'll use it. If you're gonna date, then know that every time you do, your heart's probably gonna break. I mean, there are only 2 options that can end a dating

relationship. Seriously, there are only 2 options. Can't find 1 more option; just these 2. When you date, your 2 choices for ending the dating part of the relationship are:

1. Breaking up
2. Marriage

If you aren't ready for #2, then I've got shocking news: look out for #1. If you don't live on your own yet and can't afford to pay rent, insurance, car expenses, etc., then seriously don't sweat #2. It won't be happenin' for a while, so that leaves you with option #1. Check out chapter 1 in the book I wrote with Justin Lookadoo called *Dateable: Are You? Are They?* for more info on why the broken heart is the most likely outcome of a dating relationship.

Heart breaker. Even if your heart *never* breaks, which I seriously doubt, you will more than likely end up hurting someone else along the way. It's a fact of life that when a relationship ends, someone, if not two someones, is (or are) going to be hurting. There is no way around the pain. Dating is a risky business for both you and your dated one.

4. **Stunts your growth.** Just as much as dating can teach you about yourself if done right, it can also stunt your growth if done, well, wrong! This might be a reason your parents might not want you to date. Right now you are learning who you are. You are in the process of becoming an independent person, and if you throw another person in the mix and the relationship happens to be dysfunctional in any way, you run the risk of stunting your growth by putting all your energy into the other person. So be careful. Before you date, get right with yourself. Know who you are and what you want, and don't let anyone control you or change you into what they want you to be.

5. **Distracts you from your passion.** You have a mission in life. You might not know what it is yet, but you might never know if you keep your mind on the opposite sex all day long. You need time to figure out who you are and who you were meant to be, and dating can get in the way of that if you let it. So don't get too obsessed about finding someone until you've found your purpose and your passion. Spend your energy designing your life and figuring out what you want to do before you dive into a serious relationship. 🗯

This Ain't Your Parents' World No More

In 1950, most girls waited until age 20 to get married. In 2002, the age for most marriages was 25.

In the old days, times were much simpler, and it was normal for people to get married very young. No one was shocked. Lives went on. Divorce was not even an option. But things have changed since your parents were young. Like it or not, people in your generation are waiting longer to get married.

One of the reasons is that girls have plans and dreams like no other time. People pretty much expect girls to go to college and pursue careers, whereas in the old days girls went to college to pursue a man. Now girls want to live life before settling down. And if they settle down too soon, they might feel cheated later in life when they see other girls zipping off to Europe, running corporations, and living their dreams. And guys, well, guys are different too. It used to be that at 18 they moved out of the house and started their lives, either in college or work. But now you find guys who are 23 and still living at home like a teenager. This stunted growth doesn't do much to help marriages. Until guys grow up and become men, with their own homes and their own lives, they won't know what to do with a wife. All that to say that for better or worse, times have changed, things are different, and that makes dating and marriage different too. It means that you probably won't get married right out of high school or even college. And that means that dating is more of an experience of the opposite sex and less of a courtship for marriage.

In the past guys turned into men at 18 or even earlier and were ready for the responsibility of a family and all that goes with it. And when girls turned into women at 18 or earlier and were ready to give up everything to take care of a family, it made sense to get married young. People were ready to be adults much earlier than we are now. The truth is that the majority of 25-year-olds today would tell you they don't feel like adults yet. In fact, in a recent poll most people stated that they think adulthood begins at 26.* That's a huge change from past generations. And that's a reason why most people are waiting longer to get married. They are waiting till they grow up.

So before you get serious about relationships, it's a good idea to figure out if you're one who wants to put off marriage or dive right in. Here are some things to think about before you choose your option.

Why Wait to Get Married?

Get a sense of who you are. Part of the cool thing about your college years is that you get to learn more about who you are, what you like, and what you want. It's a good time to explore things and figure out what turns your crank. You will change your ideas of what you want to do, who you want to be, and who you want to marry a bazillion times between high school graduation and college graduation. And these years in between are the times when you can learn the most. Then, when you are sure that you know who you are, you can be sure that you can find a mate who's perfect for you. Taking time to get to know you is a definite bonus for later in life. It saves all kinds of heartache.

Figure out what you want to do. Not a lot of teenagers know exactly what they want to do when they graduate from high school, and those who do probably don't want anything to get in the way of that. So the time between moving away from your parents and getting married is a good time to figure out what your purpose in life is and to find out what you want to do with yourself.

* Stephanie K. Taylor, "Delaying Adulthood," *Washington Times*, August 15, 2003, http://www.washtimes.com/culture/20030814-085130-5080r.htm.

What do you do best? After you figure out what you want to do, it's kinda good to find out if you can do it or not. I mean, are you any good at it? If you think of something you'd love to do and then when you try it you just aren't any good, then you gotta go back to the drawing board to find something else. Your single years give you time to do that without messing up the life of your mate. It's a lot easier to change your plans when you are single than when you have another person to consider.

Where do you want to go, live, move, and so on? I used my college years as a time to explore the world. I moved all over the place. I didn't have to get anyone to agree with me; I just decided where I wanted to go and went. It was the best experience I could have had. It made me into a strong adult and taught me a lot about the world. If you wait to get married, you can explore the world a lot more and find out what you really want and where you really fit.

Get autonomous. Don't go from your parents' home to your married home. You can't be truly who you are till you are your own person, and you do that on your own. If you don't get autonomous—that is, independent—before you get married, you run the risk of ending up really needy. Your mate becomes your new parent. Yuck! Who wants to marry a little kid? If you rush from home to marriage you miss out on the op to get that inner confidence, self-assuredness, and independence to make your future marriage work. When you feel unsatisfied by your work and your friends, you start rushing around looking for the next dysfunctional person to fill you. And that isn't their job; it's God's. So build your own life and your own support structure so you won't make a god of your mate. People who are fulfilled when they are single make better mates in marriage. Sure, you can make it if you get married before this happens, but you're going to have a lot of strain on the relationship that might not be there if you work out who you are before you tie the knot.

Find the one you really want, not just someone who will do. Every time you date well and then clearly see that the person isn't the one, you get one step closer to finding the one. And if you can learn how to have healthy relationships with healthy breakups, then you get better and better at being the person your future mate for life needs.

When it comes to dating there are all kinds of ops. There are lots of reasons that it can be good for you and lots of reasons that it can be bad. Like I said before, the Bible doesn't tell us anything about dating in and of itself, but it has all you need to know about God, purpose, and relationships. Talk it out with God, study his Word, find out your purpose and your goals, and then decide if dating is best for you or if waiting is your cup of tea. The thing to remember is that we are all different. No one way is right for everyone. So don't pick your way and then slam everyone who does it another way; you don't have a biblical leg to stand on. Dating is a choice each person needs to make. The main thing to remember is that dating is for people who are looking to get married. It's prep for wedded bliss. It's the way you find your partner. And the Bible is very clear that once married, always married. Divorce is not an option, so choose wisely, young grasshopper.

Getting a Little Spiritual

In the book *Dateable* we said that God made guys to be leaders when it comes to relationships, and a lot of people wondered where we got that. So before we go on, let's get into this idea a little more. It wasn't just something we made up. It's an idea that many a biblical scholar supports, so let's see if I can't help decipher some of their highfalutin language. You see, the Bible doesn't have a lot to say about dating since, like I said, in the olden days you didn't date, you let your parents do the picking, but it does have some stuff to say about marriage. And since marriage is the ultimate goal of dating, we can understand the process (dating) more by understanding the outcome (marriage). This next section is a way of understanding how God designed the concept of marriage.

In 1 Corinthians 11:3, the apostle Paul says that God made the husband to be the leader of the wife: *"But I want you to understand that the head of every man is Christ, the head of a wife is her husband, and the head of Christ is God"* (ESV). Now, lots of people laugh at this verse. They say, "How out-of-date. This can't be true." And some even say that it's not something that applies to us today but applied only to the church of Paul's day. In fact, tons of couples around the world think marriage is 50-50, with no leader. And some even think it's just up to the strongest personality to lead, and sometimes that means the woman leads. And life goes on. The world even tells us that women should take the lead. And every fashion mag out there teaches us how to do it.

But the way I see it, God made men like oranges and women like peaches. Both are round, orange fruits, both equally good for you, and still they're obviously different. But some think that while we were created different, once we accept Christ into our lives we all become pears. Equal, the same. Now, you might have different experiences than me and think that guys and girls are 100 percent equal, liking the same things, wanting the same stuff, and acting the same way, but that hasn't been my experience. I see guys acting totally differently than girls and wanting totally different things. Not many of my guy friends get all excited to go on vacation to a spa and get manicures, massage, and pedicures all day long, and not so many of my girlfriends dream about hunting trips and boxing camp. So instead of getting into a discussion on fruit salad, let me just say this—I believe that according to the Bible, God is calling guys to take the lead with the gentle confidence and the servant attitude of Christ, and girls are called to allow them to lead just as Christ allowed the Father to lead in his life.

The truth is that 50 percent of all marriages end in divorce, and I ask myself *Why?* See, the way I figure it, if what you're doing isn't working, then maybe you need to change. Over the past 50 years we've seen the role of the woman "evolve" into a very empowered, controlling, leading position. We applaud a woman's freedom to be just like a man. And then we wonder why marriages are failing and families are falling apart. As I search for the answers to these tough questions in God's Word, I start to wonder, *What if we've gotten it wrong?* What if God's Word isn't a *description* of a time in the early church but really a *prescription* for living in *every* church, in *every* time? What if what 1 Corinthians says about the role of men and women in relationship is God's design for a healthy relationship, even for today? Would that change the way we think about the roles of husband and wife?

I can tell you right now that I have girlfriends who strongly disagree with me here and others who totally agree. It's a point of contention even among Christian women: when it comes to relationships, does God see the man as the ultimate head of his wife? I have to say yes, and you might disagree, but in the end, when your dating relationship ends in marriage, you will have to decide how you are going to deal with God's commands for man and woman. (If you want to do more research on this, check out Ephesians 5:21–25; 1 Corinthians 11:3; 1 Peter 3:3–6; Colossians 3:18–19).

Note for Girls: You can choose to practice for marriage—i.e., date—in any way that you want. You can date ignoring the things you've just read and then see how you fare or you can practice living according to this "new" idea now and see if when it's time to follow your man you won't be really good at it. Like some sports guy said, you play the way you practice. So if you're like me and you'd like to see if God's Word for the early church doesn't work just as well for you, then read on. We have a lot of learning to do. How do we help guys to lead? How do we stop the urge to take over like Eve did? How do we learn to be attractive to a guy who knows deep down that a girl who follows is for some reason more attractive than a girl who leads him?

It's simple, really: we stop taking over in the dating relationship. We let guys do the asking out, the calling, and the planning. They were programmed to take charge, not to be taken charge of. I know, it's so hard to wait for a guy to get a clue. Sometimes it seems like they will never make a move, and the only option seems to be to make it for them. But wait a sec. What if I said there was another way? What if there were a healthy, godly way to be the girl of his dreams and help him figure out that it's time to make a move? Well, wouldn't you know it but there is a way, and you don't need to wait any longer to find it out. Being a girl of mystery and the girl of his dreams is easier than you thought.

Note for Guys: Hear this, guys: You can choose to practice for marriage—i.e., date—in any way that you want. You can date ignoring the things you've just read about guys leading and let your crush take the lead on everything. Then if and when you marry her, you can learn a new set of rules and try to take back leadership from a girl who has gotten really used to leading you. Or you can practice living according to this "new" idea now and see if when it's time to lead your family you won't be really good at it. Like they say in sports, you play the way you practice. So if you'd like to see if God's Word for the early church doesn't work just as well for you, then read on. We have a lot of learning to do. How do you take the lead in a relationship that isn't marriage? How do you act like the man God wants you to be? How do you get girls to let you be the leader and lay off on the controlling stuff? It might be easier than you think.

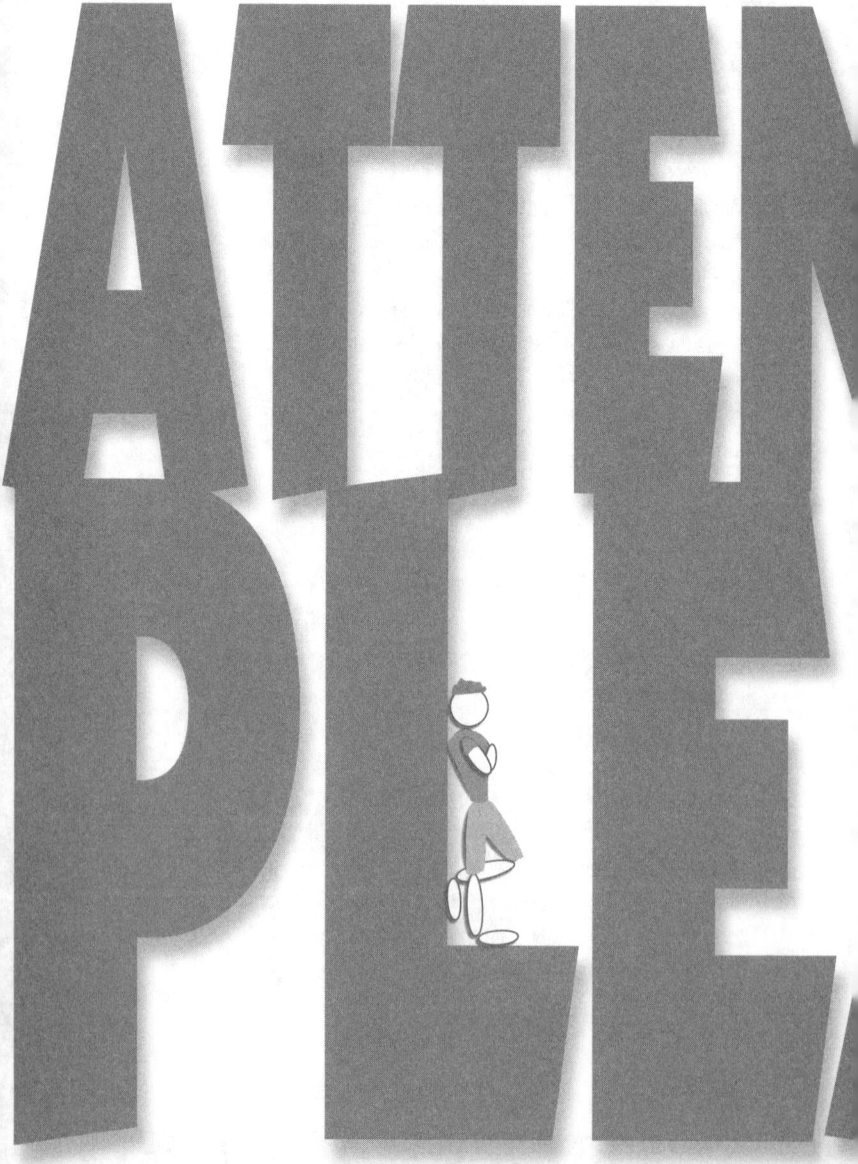
ATTEN
PLE

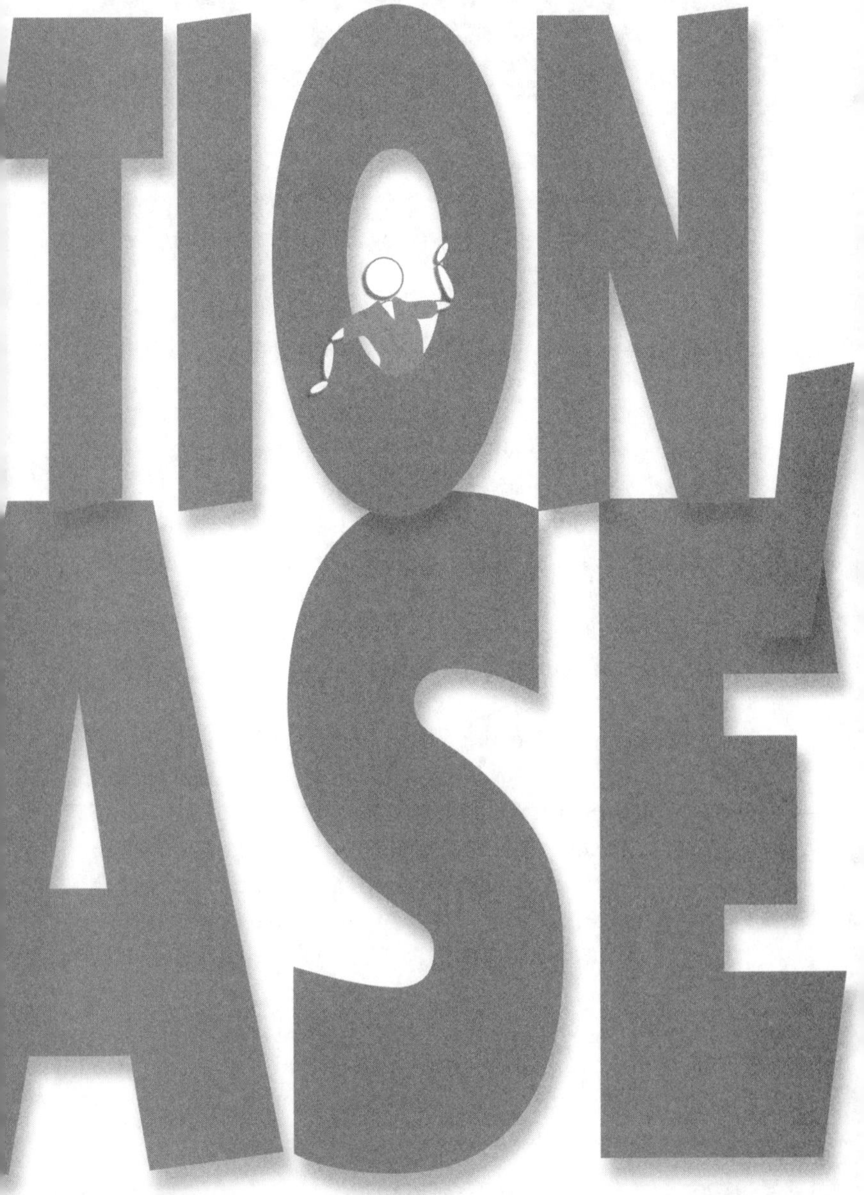
TION,
ASE

Flirting sometimes gets a bad rap. And if used improperly it can be a manipulative tool in the hands of a crazed guy or girl. But if used properly it is a sweet way of telling someone that you think they are special. It's really an art form that allows people communicate affection and acceptance in playful and fun ways. Most people love to be flirted with, because it means that someone thinks they are interesting, funny, or just plain good looking. It builds up people's self-esteem and gives them energy. Flirting is the best way for 2 people to know if they like each other in the same way. It's a clue that tells you if you should approach for more or just walk away. Not returning the flirting is a good way to tell someone kindly that you aren't interested. And of course returning the flirting is a good way for us girls to show interest without pressuring the guy to get moving and ask us out. It makes us more attractive and guys more appreciated.

But flirting can be tough if you don't know what you are doing. In fact, it can be downright dangerous in the hands of an amateur. So the following pages are here to shed a little light on the subject of flirting. Please note that the flirting we are proposing here is flirting with intent. **Never flirt with someone you don't want to date.** People who do that are called a tease. They use flirting to make themselves feel better, and they give flirting a bad rap. Flirting is simply non-verbal communication between two people who like one another enough to pursue a relationship. When you flirt with someone you would never consider dating, you are being cruel and unkind.

Also note that flirting, as I'm defining it in the pages that follow, isn't used for sexual advances or innuendo. It is simply a gentle and sweet signal to another that you are interested in them and that taking the next step is appropriate.

No Flirt Zone

Think of a world where flirting is prohibited.

For guys it would be a nightmare. They would have no idea who liked them, who would accept a date, and who would leave them to burn. Asking a girl out is a scary proposition, and without clear evidence that she wants him to ask her, he runs the risk of being shot down. Think of a girl who is asked out by a guy she would never be caught dead with. She has no attraction to him and no desire to go out with him, but he's asked her, and now she is left with the difficult challenge of telling him no without hurting him—or, harder yet, telling him no so he gets it. Some guys can be so doggone aggressive that they won't leave a girl alone, and then the agony starts. But flirting to the rescue! When guys start to understand that flirting is a girl's way of hinting that she'd like to be asked out and when girls understand that flirting is only reserved for guys you want to date, rejection problem solved.

In a world without flirting, guys are left without a clue. Ask any guy and he'll say he has no idea what women are thinking or what they want, so imagine how much more difficult it would be without the flirting process. Flirting is an essential step in the dating and mating process. Throwing it out because some people abuse it is throwing the proverbial baby out with the bathwater. Ouch! And who wants all the crying?

OK, i like this guy, and he flirts with everyone,
but i guess he flirts with me more. everyone
tells me that they think he likes me, but i don't
know. sometimes we talk and have a lot of fun but
sometimes when i'm around him it can be awkward. i
dunno if he likes me and is scared or doesn't like
me and is uncomfortable b/c his friends bug him
and me about it. i need help!

—Kristi

it's wrong for a guy to flirt with a girl when he
has a gurlfriend. my b/f flirts with all these
gurls that go to our school and there is no way to
tell if he is cheating on me or not! can you tell
me what i can do to dump him but not make it so
obvious that i'm doing it?

—Jennifer

OK, this flirting is a confusing subject . . .
I don't know what to do! I flirt a lot but not
with just people I like but with EVERYONE I see.
Flirting makes me attract the people I don't want
and push away the people I do want! So I don't
know what to do. . . . HELP, SOMEONE!

—Crystal

Why do girls flirt when they have a boyfriend? all
i have to say is it's just wrong to flirt with
other guys when you're dating, 'cuz it's just like
cheating in a guy's eyes. If I ever saw my g/f
flirting with a guy it would kill me. I wouldn't
date any girl who ever thought it was OK to flirt
while they have a b/f. I'm sorry but I'm sure God
doesn't look down and say that's OK.

—Jason

Flirting takes skill, and it also takes love and kindness. Never use flirting in the following situations:

- when you have a boyfriend/girlfriend already
- when you don't like the guy/girl you are flirting with
- when it's all you do (be picky; don't flirt with everyone or everyone will be confused)
- when you are just being cruel
- when you want someone to do something for you
- when the person has a boyfriend/girlfriend
- when he/she is way too old for you
- when it is overly sexual (guys are easily turned on, so keep it clean!)

Flirting has to do with motive. In the following pages you are going to learn a lot more about flirting, but make sure your motive is pure, 'cuz God sees right through it, and if you are using flirting for any of these bad things you will be judged. "All a man's ways seem innocent to him, but motives are weighed by the LORD" (Proverbs 16:2). Flirting can be fun and good for relationships; just make sure you are using it in a godly way.

Guys, you have your own section. Flip to page 47.

Girls Flirting Madly:

All About Being a Girl and Flirting

Yeah, flirting is, of course, fun for us girls. and no, u don't/shouldn't do it to just anyone. You should put your time into the people you care about—as in flirt with the boys you have feelings for! . . . not just anyone is worth your time, hun—but that special someone is.

—Emmie

EVERY girl has the ability to flirt. it's like in our blood or something. So be friendly and if you want him to know for sure you like him flip your hair a little and let him catch you taking a glance at him. Don't chase him, let him chase you, but you gotta be noticeable and different from the rest. Just turn on the flirting and let God take care of the rest!

—Beach Girl

A GIRL QUIZ

1. At lunch your crush sits at the table across from yours, giving you a clear shot to his eyes, so you:

   a. keep your eyes on your friends; you don't want to give him any ideas
   b. look at him several times while you eat, only looking down after he sees you catching a peek
   c. smile at him and mouth the words, "How are you?"

2. You see your crush coming down the hall. You:

   a. back up just in time for him to run into you and say, "Oh, I'm sorry, my bad."
   b. look down in embarrassment and try not to let him see you blush
   c. grab his arm as he walks by and say, "Aren't you going to say hi?"

3. It's game night and your crush is playing, so your game plan is:

   a. to go with your friends and wave at him from the stands
   b. to take signs with his name all over them and wave them as you shout "GO"
   c. you aren't really into sports, so you decide to go to a movie with your girlfriend

more

4. After school you see your crush standing with a bunch of guys by his car, so you:

- a. go the other way; you don't want to talk to him with all those guys around
- b. walk up to the group and say, "Which one of you can drive me home today?"
- c. walk over to him, grab his arm, and whisper something in his ear right before you walk off

5. In class they are choosing work groups for your new project. Your crush is the one choosing for his group, so you:

- a. make strong eye contact so that he sees you want him to pick you for his group
- b. look down and try to be cute as you bite your lower lip; you know he'll see you and have to pick you
- c. raise your hand and shout, "Pick me, pick me!"

6. It's the first day of class and when you get there your crush has already taken a seat. You:

- a. pick one right next to him and start a convo with him
- b. pick one a couple seats away; you don't want to be too obvious
- c. sit right in front of him; that way he'll see you every single day.

7. At the dance you spot your crush across the room, so you:

- a. get a girlfriend to move over there with you to dance right in front of him
- b. go over and ask him to dance
- c. take a seat and wait for him to see you and ask you to dance

8. In P.E. you are on opposite teams for flag football, so you:

a. try to get him as your man so you can chase him all over the field

b. play tough athlete and start bad-mouthing him like the opponent that you are

c. act like you aren't dying inside to just skip the flags and tackle him!

Scoring

1. a = 1, b = 2, c = 3   **5.** a = 2, b = 1, c = 3
2. a = 2, b = 1, c = 3   **6.** a = 2, b = 1, c = 3
3. a = 2, b = 3, c = 1   **7.** a = 2, b = 3, c = 1
4. a = 1, b = 2, c = 3   **8.** a = 3, b = 2, c = 1

8–14: Shy Girl How will he ever know that you like him if you don't show him? Guys are slow; they need signals. They need little hints that if they asked you out you'd say yes, aka flirting. So if you're crushing on a guy, for goodness' sake, a few hints please!

15–18: Flirting Queen You got it down, girl. Let the guy know you are crushing on him. Not too obvious, but very flirty. Well done. People love to be flirted with; it's a sign of acceptance and appreciation. So keep up the flirtation and you'll make it easy for the one you want to ask you out.

19–24: Flirt Alert! Beware, your flirting might be running amuck. Subtlety might bring you more success. Don't scare the guy off with your affection. Slow down. Make yourself a little less obvious and a little more of a challenge.

How to Get His ATTENTION

Don't Chase Him More Than He's Chasing You

So you wanna chase a guy? Fine, just follow this one simple rule: don't chase him more than he's chasing you. You heard me. Don't get all in front of him in the chase thing. Or, I guess, *do* get in front of him, with him behind you chasing you, if you can catch the image. A guy needs to feel like he's the hunter, he's the one chasing the prize. When you take over and do all the chasin', he might be flattered, but in the end he feels just plain empty, bored, and all that stuff. He thinks, "Hmm, there's nothing to do here; she's doing it all. What use am I?" He decides he's of no use, so he moves on to a girl who'll let him play a more active role and chase her. So no chasin' him harder than he's chasin' you. It just don't work.

If you still aren't buying this and are screaming at me like a wild-eyed feminist, "Archaic simpleton! Women have just as much right to pursue a guy! Crawl out of the

warning Don't chase him more than he's chasing you.

34

ice ages!" then let me ask you just one question: Do you live based on the world's agenda or God's agenda? If you are brave enough to choose the latter, then bravo and hold on, 'cuz it gets wild for us Bible thumpers. Girls have a lot of Qs about how they should act with guys, and rightfully so, because like I've said, there isn't too much in Scripture about dating and all that. But what there *is*, is a bit of info on the desired outcome of dating, and by that I mean marriage. To find out what God wants you to do in your dating life, find out what he wants in your married life. Remember, dating is just practice for marriage. So get it right in practice and the game will go great, so to speak. The Bible is really clear to all who are brave enough to really look that the man is the head of the family just like Christ is the head of the church (Eph. 5:21–24; Col. 3:18–19; 1 Peter 3:1). But he can handle it. It's when girls try to take over and run things that the real pressure hits. If a woman tries to lead her husband, she is making it impossible for him to fulfill his God-given duty. So girls, we need to learn and we need to learn *now* how to slow down and let guys lead. Let them practice being the one who takes initiative; let them learn what it means to be the leader. If you don't, you are only helping to stunt their spiritual growth and their development as true men of God.

Wives, submit to your own husbands, as to the Lord. For the husband is the head of the wife even as Christ is the head of the church, his body, and is himself its Savior. Now as the church submits to Christ, so also wives should submit in everything to their husbands.

Ephesians 5:22–24 ESV

Okay, I hear you saying, "That's all well and good, but how do I do that? I'm good with the idea of the guy being the leader and all. I just have no idea what that looks like." Stay with me, 'cuz that's exactly where we're going.

"But He Won't Lead"

I know he might not seem like a leader right now, but that's where you come in. You have to *let* him lead, give him space and the opp to do something. Don't take control away from him if he is slow on the draw. If guys don't see an opening that they can fill, they get lazy and comfortable letting you do all the leading. If you choose the restaurant, where you sit, when you leave, and everything else, he has nothing to do. Suddenly you are defining the relationship, all its ups and downs, and the guy has control of nothing. Then before you know it he wants out, and you have no idea why. For him, it's because he's suddenly realized that he's been taken somewhere he didn't want to go. And he wants out. If you let him lead the relationship from the beginning, he'll take it where he wants to go and won't be so apt to bail when things get serious (see *Define the Relationship*, page 80).

How to Let Him Chase You More

In *Dateable* we talk about this idea of letting him chase you in the chapter called "Girls, Shut Up and Be Mysterious." Girls who have read *Dateable* have sent me all kinds of comments like "Okay, so how do I become mysterious?" This, my girls, is my tried and true answer on how to make yourself that mystery girl that guys fall head over heels for.

He calls more – When it comes to the phone, slow it down. He needs
to be the one making the most phone calls. Sure, after you are going out
for a while you can call him. You are close enough. But just watch yourself
and make sure you aren't the one making the most effort. It's a chasing
thing. In order for him to feel like *he's* chasing *you*, he needs to feel like
he's making the most phone calls. So if he calls and you are out, you don't
have to return *every* phone call, because you don't want to be calling him
as much as he calls you. Relax. If you guys are close and on good terms
and you don't call back right away, he'll call again, believe me. I'm not
really into rules, but here's a good etiquette gauge for phone calls:

> The **50 percent rule**: for every 2 calls he makes, you give him 1, if
> you really like him.
>
> If you aren't sure how much you like him, **go for 1 in 3** return phone
> calls.
>
> If you're not interested at all, **don't keep calling him back**, even if
> you are bored. You will give him the wrong idea. When you see
> him at school, say hi first and just chat for a second. Keep the
> convo on school and then move on. Be sure not to flirt.

He says more – I know you love to talk, and you probably talk more than
him, but keep your mouth shut more than him when it comes to affection.
Let him be the first to tell you how much he cares. Let him chase you with
his words. You can return the favor, just don't do it *first* or more often.

He gives more – It's a weird thing with girls, but we feel more loved
when boys give us things. Gifts, flowers, attention, all that stuff means
major points for the guy, so we think that it's the same for him getting
stuff from us. But it isn't. How odd, I know! But guys get more of a rush
from doing things for girls than they do from getting things from girls.
So if you are heavy on the giving—cards, gifts, back rubs—you aren't
doing yourself any favors. He isn't giving you love points for your gifts.

He might think they are nice and all, but you score much more on the love Richter scale when you graciously accept the things he does for, and gives *to*, you.

Use body language – Guys love a confident girl. You might not really feel too confident, but that's okay. You can appear confident even if you don't feel like it. It's all about body language. Who wants to be alone with someone who looks like they don't even like to be alone with themselves? So here's what you do to look like you actually like yourself and think you are fun to be with:

> *Stand straight* – Keep your back straight and stand with your feet no farther than 6 inches apart and your toes pointed in a little bit.
>
> *Look him in the eye* – Don't be too shy to look him in the eye. That means you think you are worthy of him and he's worthy of you. You don't have to stare; just look for a couple seconds and then look down. He'll get the picture.
>
> *Talk* – I know it's hard to talk when a guy is drop dead gorgeous, but you gotta do it. Don't clam up. Make small talk. Say hi. Ask him how he is. Talking is a good thing, and it encourages a guy to talk to you more.
>
> *Touch your hair* – You probably already do this without even knowing it, but it's a sure sign to a guy that you are interested. Toss it from one side to the other. Smooth it down. Play with it a little and he'll get the hint. But don't act like you're starring in some kind of remake of *Charlie's Angels* and over-flip. That kind of overacting only works for Cameron Diaz.
>
> *Copycat* – Watch his body language and make yours the same. If he has his hand on his face, put your hand on your face. It is a

subconscious way to say, "I agree with you. I'm on your side." And subconsciously he'll get it.

Touch him a little – If you really think a guy is for you, the final stage is to invade his personal space. It doesn't take much, just a brush of your hand on his arm or a bump up against him with your shoulder. Anything that starts to break down the invisible barrier between you is a good flirting technique.

Catch his eye – The best way to catch anyone's eye is to have something unique about you. That might be a really funky scarf or hat or a bizarre bracelet. Anything that the guy can use as a conversation starter is always a good idea. Besides, it builds your quirky factor, and quirky is good.

Compliment him – It's polite and just good manners to compliment people, but it also tells a guy that you are interested. So don't overdo it, but do make sure to tell him something about him that you admire or appreciate. He'll love it. (See *How to Compliment* on page 40.)

Fearless – The best flirt is one who is self-confident and fearless, willing to risk rejection just to see what will happen. So don't worry about how the guy will take it—most will love it, I promise. Flirting with someone is one of the biggest compliments you can give them. And if for some odd reason they are anti-flirting, then oh well. Nothing ventured, nothing gained. Laugh it off and move on. Besides, it will be a great story to tell your friends. We all need something to laugh at about ourselves; it helps make us human.

How to Compliment

Guys and girls want to be complimented in different ways. Don't compliment the way you want to be complimented, because it won't make as much sense to the opposite sex. The basic thing you need to know is that girls like to be complimented on *who* they are. Their beauty, their brains, their talents, stuff about them as a person. But **guys would rather be complimented on <u>what they did</u> than who they are.**

Not makin' any sense? I know, it was strange to me when I first figured it out too. So compare these charts and maybe you'll start to see the differences.

Compliments for Guys
That was such a great idea.
I never would have thought of that.
Love your shirt.
I'm having an awesome time.
I had so much fun tonight.
I had a great time talking with you yesterday.
That movie was great.

Compliments for Girls
You are so smart.
I love how creative you are.
You look amazing in that dress.
You're so awesome.
You are so much fun to be with.
You are so great to talk to.
You always pick the best movies.

Ah, the subtleties of being a woman of mystery! But trust me, girls, if you get this stuff right you'll be able to charm his socks off!

| hint | When you genuinely compliment people, they like you more. |

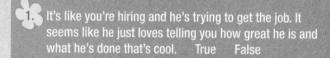

1. It's like you're hiring and he's trying to get the job. It seems like he just loves telling you how great he is and what he's done that's cool. True False

2. Whenever he sees you, he smiles and looks you right in the eyes. True False

3. On a couple of occasions you have caught him checking out your body—not like a perv, but slyly looking you up and down. True False

4. He IMs you a lot. He always seems to be online when you are. True False

5. He calls you just to chat. True False

6. He asks you a lot of questions about yourself. True False

7. He seems really interested in what you have to say. True False

8. He offers to do really nice things like carry your books, give you a ride, and help you with homework. True False

scoring

Scoring

Add up how many "True" answers you have: _____

1–3 True: Not so sure he's into you, girl. Sorry to be the bearer of bad news, but either you have a really shy guy or he just isn't into you like that. Either way, don't try to fix it. Let him be. Let him do what he will do. Be strong and one day a guy will find you to be the dream that you are.

4–5 True: He just might dig you. He's a dude, and what do they know about girls? But the signs seem to be pointing in a good direction. He's making some kind of attempt. It might be just for friendship, but find out more by returning his flirting and see where it goes.

6–8 True: He's sold. The guy is gaga for you, in case you were totally clueless. You are making his life wonderful. Keep up the flirting and let him take it where he will, but I'm pretty sure a date is in your future.

The Opposite of Flirting:
What Turns Him Off?

Girls who complain all the time – If you wanna turn a guy off, then complain about something. Ugh! What a pain in the bleep! Complaining just ain't cool. No one wants to hear how horrible things are, especially not guys. Here's a little secret: when you complain about something to a guy, you actually run the risk of making him feel like you are unhappy with him. Guys can take complaints about something they've given you, thought of, or even done with you as a direct hit. Even if you're complaining about things that don't involve him, newsflash: guys are obsessed with fixing things! It's a part of guyness. If you are constantly complaining about things, he gets exhausted trying to fix them or frustrated that he can't. So shut up and keep your whining for Mommy and your teddy bear.

Girls who don't need a guy – I know it seems weird to girls, but believe me when I tell you that guys like to be needed. It's one more part of guyness. If you need no one, you have no purpose in guyville. That's why guys want to be part of a team, why dads get depressed when they don't have a job, and why guys aren't interested in girls who can do it all themselves. If you don't need him for anything, then you don't need him.

Girls who need him too much – I know, I just said that a guy needs to be needed, but if you need him *too* much, that's just as bad as not needing him at all. Part of why you date and wait before you get married is so that you have time to become independent. You have time to become who you are. If you go from needing Daddy, to needing a guy like a daddy, you can wear a guy out.

Girls who tell him everything – "Blah, blah, blah." This is what he hears when you talk too much. Don't tell him everything; it's too much for a guy to handle. Best policy? Just tell him good stuff. Make conversation, but keep the intimate, uncomfortable, or way too personal stuff to yourself. I know this seems like such a foreign concept to us girls. I mean, we bond by talking! The more I tell you about me, the more I like you and the more you like me. That's just how it works. But check out 2 guys hanging out. What do they do together? It gives you a good clue about what they like to do. Do they sit around chatting about their deepest fears? Do they analyze each other's dreams? Do they encourage each other about their fat bottoms and flabby arms? Do they in any way spend their time communicating the way we do? Seems like such a stupid question, I know. But you really need to think about this one. When guys are alone together, they avoid deep convo and go straight for competition, games, sports. For the most part guys don't bond by sharing deep emotions. So now why do you think that suddenly, when they are with you, everything they are, think, and feel goes out the window and they become, well, girls? Listen, guys are not girls. Therefore, you can't talk to them like girls. Think about what they like instead of what you like. Novel concept! Give others what they want instead of what you want. And give your mouth a break.

Girls who always think there is a problem – There's just something about us girls that makes us wanna make everyone happy, so when you sense that someone is bummed or upset, your number one goal is to fix it. Trouble is, the way you fix it is by talking about it—and most often, too much. If there is a problem, most of the time a guy will work it out on his own unless he really needs to bring it to your attention. I'm not saying don't ever ask if there is a problem. It's just that when you think that every little thing is a sign that he is upset, you aren't right; you're just annoying.

Girls who backstab other girls – You think they aren't watching, but they are. When you go psycho on another girl and do all you can to bring her down, it shows. And it ain't a pretty sight. You might feel good about it, and your girlfriends might applaud you, but to a guy you just look like a witch.

Girls who are jealous – Jealousy isn't a pretty color on anyone. So if you are jealous, keep it to yourself. Jealousy just means that you don't think you're as good as the other girl. That makes you look bad, insecure. Try to keep the "mean green" within you under wraps unless the guy is just totally out of hand in his flaunting of his "other girls"—and in that case then just dump him. Don't try to use jealousy to change him. 🐾

Why Guys Like Girls

Guys tell us why they like girls so much:

1. You always smell so good.

2. You look really cute when you eat.

3. You need help with stuff.

4. You laugh at my jokes.

5. You are soft.

6. You are sweet.

7. You care.

8. You giggle.

9. You blush.

10. Your hair is soft.

How to Make a Guy **Smile**

- **Be yourself** – Most guys can see through your fakeness, and even if they can't, the best you is the real you. So be yourself!

- **Appreciate him** – Say thanks for stuff he does. Make him feel important and useful.

- **Eat with him** – Don't order a salad and barely pick at it. Eat like you mean it—guys love that.

- **Laugh at him** – Guys love to be funny, so laugh, even at his stupid jokes.

- **Don't complain about stuff** – Whine, whine, whine, no one likes a whiner. And remember, "Do everything without complaining" (Philippians 2:14).

- **Be easy to get along with** – Pretty self-explanatory. It's also called loving your neighbor as yourself. Check out 1 Corinthians 13 if you need help on loving.

- **Smile** – Guys love a smile. It means you are happy, and they love to make you happy.

- **Be adventurous** – Guys are really looking for a girl who will play with them, so be daring. Go rock climbing, play basketball, get sweaty. Don't be quick to say no to stuff you've never done. Outdoor adventure can be a blast. So cut your nails and get in shape, and he'll love ya!

- **Flirt a little** – If you like him, then show it. Be a girl. Flip your hair, touch his arm, make him feel special.

- **Let him be a guy** – I know you can do things on your own, but when he's around, let him do some things. Let him get the door, open the ketchup, or carry your books. Guys love to be needed.

Guys and Flirting:

How to Take the Lead in Things

I would like the guy 2 flirt once in a while but not all the time b/c that's usually the girls job. guys can flirt too, but usually they don't flirt. I wish he would flirt some so I would know if he likes me.

—Christiangirl

i hate to say it, but when the guy instigates the flirting, it is SO much more fun. i don't know, maybe it is because he is showing interest in me first, but it makes it easier and funner for me to flirt back. is that heinous?

—Yourockmysocks

Communication

I know girls *love* to talk, but don't expect her to carry the load when it comes to connecting. As the leader you call her, you chase her, you ask her out. When you call and she isn't there, leave a message to let her know you'll call back later. Don't be a wimp and ask her to call you back so she has to be the one to initiate. Be a gentleman and take the lead. I've told the girls not to call you more than you call them. Please send your thank-you cards to P.O. Box 1234, Dateable City, Anywhere USA, because I just saved you a great deal of heartache, or at least earache. Now don't let me down by sitting around waiting for *her* to call *you*. It ain't supposed to work that way.

Giving

Girls feel totally loved when they get gifts. Now, you don't have to shower us with presents, but a gift here and there speaks volumes. So be sure that you take the lead when it comes to giving. Don't you dare let her outgive you, or she'll be back into a leading position. Leading means being the one who initiates things—calling, talking, and giving.

DTR: Define the Relationship

Don't expect her to do it. She isn't in charge of the relationship. If she is truly *Dateable*, she is waiting for *you* to define the relationship. This can be very tricky. Don't do it too early. Watch for signs from her. You'll know when the time is right to up the stakes and let her know how you feel. Just be sure not to sit around waiting for her to do it. That's totally not cool. For more info on this, go to *The DTR*, page 80.

Flirting With Girls:
How-to's That Really Work

The main thing in pursuing a girl is that you don't wait for her to make the first move. Flirting correctly will help you to know if the chances are good that she will say yes, but in the end you are the one who has to risk all and ask—that is, lead.

When you find a girl you like and really want to approach for a date, you need to get the signals going. Asking a girl out cold turkey is kind of a shock to the system. First she needs to see that you are interested and be allowed to show you she is interested as well. So slow the boat down and try some of these things before you dive in and ask her to do something with you.

Notice her Girls love to be noticed. It makes them feel really special. So make sure she sees you noticing her. Don't act like some kind of construction worker on break, but do sneak a peek at her so she catches you.

Look at her eyes If you can't look a girl in the eyes, you can't get her attention. Girls are all about eyes; they love 'em, and they love it when you look them in the eye.

Be clean and smell good Smells are really important to girls. They get turned on by what they smell, so do your best to smell good. Take care of your teeth, check your breath, and, yes, keep your breath strips handy.

Try to get to know her Girls want to be known. They want someone to really get who they are. That means you ask her about herself, you let her talk, you let her express herself. The more she can tell you about herself, the more she'll like you.

Show that you are attracted Girls need clues. They need to know you are interested. Then in turn they will let you know they are attracted. That takes off the edge of fear about asking her out. Show her you are attracted and see how she reacts. If she is obviously cold, then she's probably not interested.

Smile at her A smile goes a long way. Everyone loves a smile. So use your smile; it speaks volumes.

Be where she is Find out what she likes and what she does and show up there. Now, don't become a stalker guy; just explore. If she obviously couldn't care less that you are there, then back off. Don't push yourself on her, but if she shows signs of liking you, you can continue to be where she is.

Give her compliments Compliments go a long way. A lot of girls don't know how to take a compliment, but that doesn't mean you should stop. Compliment straight up. Don't make up stuff, but really mean it.

Say something funny Most girls say humor is the most important thing on a guy. That means don't take yourself too seriously, even if you aren't super funny. Lighten up. Laugh. Enjoy life, and she'll love it.

Stand tall Don't stand all hunched over; she likes a man who stands up straight. It shows your confidence. Stand with your feet 6 to 10 inches apart, and point your toes out just a little.

Touch her a little Touch her lightly on the back, shoulders, or arm when you help her put her coat on, get the door for her, or guide her across the street.

Be a copycat People who agree copy each other's body language. If she is leaning forward, then lean forward. If she has her hands on her face, put your hands on your face. Subconsciously she will think you both agree, and that is good.

How to Compliment

uys and girls want to be complimented in different ways. Don't compliment the way you want to be complimented, 'cuz it won't make as much sense to the opposite sex. The basic thing you need to know is that **girls like to be complimented on *who they are.*** Their beauty, their brains, their talents, stuff about them as a person. Guys would rather be complimented on what they did than who they are.

Not makin' any sense? I know, it was strange to me when I first heard it too. So compare these charts and maybe you'll start to see the differences.

Compliments for Guys
That was such a great idea.
I never would have thought of that.
Love your shirt.
I'm having an awesome time.
I had so much fun tonight.
I had a great time talking with you yesterday.
That movie was great.

G-rated

Compliments for Girls
You are so smart.
I love how creative you are.
You look amazing in that dress.
You're so awesome.
You are so much fun to be with.
You are so great to talk to.
You always pick the best movies.

G-rated

Guys, remember to keep all your compliments G-rated. Don't talk to her about her body parts or what you want to do with them. And when you compliment, don't act like you want to get something out of it. Make it just a casual statement and don't expect anything in return.

Hints on Complimenting a Girl

Remember, when you compliment a girl it's all about *her*. So notice stuff. Girls love it when you notice their smile, their hair, their clothes. It's all about how they look and who they are as people.

> I love your smile, eyes, face, hair, accent, white teeth, soft skin, etc. . . . *(note, don't make a list, just pick 1)*

> I really like the way you do your hair, dress, decorate, paint, draw . . . *(again, pick 1)*

> You are such a good basketball player, writer, knitter, actor . . . *(must I say it again? Just use 1)*

> You dance better than anyone I know.

> You sing better than anyone on American Idol.

She Loves Me,
She Loves Me Not

How do you know she likes you?

She looks at you and looks away
She smiles at you
She giggles
She touches her hair
She bites her lip
She is always where you are
She compliments you
She touches your arm or leg lightly

If none of these are happening, then move on.
She isn't interested. 🍀

To be thought of as beautiful, inside and out

To be taken care of

To be special to someone besides her parents

Cards, love notes, smiles, kisses on the forehead, flowers, love songs

What a Girl Wants

To be treated like a princess

To make other girls jealous – i.e., to have a better boyfriend than other girls, a guy who is super sweet, caring, giving, etc.

To be heard – looked in the eye and listened to

To get sympathy for the bad stuff in her life

To be understood – just listened to, not fixed

To be protected

Her Turn-Offs

All girls are different, but there are some things that most of us just can't stand. Check out this list and make sure you aren't on it.

Guys who act like girls. Don't be overly sensitive. Don't act like your life rides on whether she likes you or not. Take it all like a man and you will be tons more attractive. She should be the more emotional one. Don't get all girly on her; let her be the female in the relationship.

Guys who are all hands. Girls like to know that you think they are hot, but when you are all hands, it's a total turn-off. It says to a girl that all you think is hot is her body, and she wants you to think her mind is hot and her heart is hot and her spirit is hot. So lay off with all the hands all over her.

Guys who never ask. Guys who are too afraid to ask her out and never even make a move turn her off slowly but surely. Mainly it's because she assumes there is something wrong with her. So step up to the plate and ask!

Guys who won't take "no" for an answer. Okay, it's cool for a guy to be the aggressor, the one who goes after the girl, but learn one thing: no means no when it comes to sex and dating. Now, no might be yes when you ask her if anything is wrong and she says no. But when you ask her if you can take off her pants and she says no, she means it. So learn to take no for an answer.

Guys who are self-absorbed. Girls love to be the center of your attention. They want to be your favorite person, so when you act like *you* are your fave person, she's out. If you want to date yourself, then by all means be into you, but if you want some lovin' from a girl, lay off with the ego trip.

Guys who fall too fast (i.e., guys who are too nice). A lot of guys say "I'm just too much of a nice guy" when they get rejected. But a lot of the time it has nothing to do with how nice you are, just how fast you are going emotionally. Don't go deeper emotionally than the girl. Girls are the more emotional sex, so when you outdo her in emotions it seems kinda creepy. She likes the excitement of not knowing everything you are thinking and feeling. (This is why so many girls say they like "bad boys." It's not because they are bad; it's just because they don't overdo the emotions.) Keep pace with her and when you think she is at a new emotional level, you can go there too. Guys, you lead the relationship, and that means it's cool for you to express your love and affection before her, but watch her and don't do anything until you are sure she will accept what you have to say.

Guys who make her be the guy. Inside of every girl is a girly girl, even if she doesn't know it. Don't make her be the guy. Carry the stuff, make the plans, pay for things, take your role so that she can take hers and find out how great it really is to be a girl.

Guys who are wimps. Protect her. Stand up for her. Be a man—not a caveman but a gentleman. Don't be afraid of her; don't be a wimp around her. Be the man you were made to be, and she'll love you for it. 💦

Girls Talk

Why We Like Guys

Girls tell guys why they like you so much:

1. Because you are so tough
2. Because you are so cute
3. Because you aren't all emotional
4. Because you protect us
5. Because you are funny
6. Because you are confident
7. Because you smell so manly

GUYS

Asking Her Out

This section is for guys, 'cuz girls, if you are asking a guy out, you are just asking for heartache. Guys are wired to be the instigators, the aggressors. Throughout time guys have been the ones who kill the animals, go to war, and save the land. They are the ones who love a challenge so much that they shape their whole lives around it. Like it or not, they were made to be the ones to ask, not you. Sure it's the 2000s, sure you *can* ask, sure it's hip to ask, but in the end it's a stupid decision that is only based on your pride and your fear of waiting for God to bring the right guy at the right time to ask you just the right way.

Girl Reminder

Dating is the training ground for marriage. And God has made it so the man is the leader of the woman. Start now to learn what that means. It doesn't mean he runs your life; it just means he takes the lead on important things like dating you.

So guys, read on. This advice is for you:

Ask her out for a specific event – Don't say, "Hey, we should go out sometime" or "You wanna do something?" Come on now, be a man, stand up and ask for what you want! "Would you like to go out to dinner next Friday night, say 7:00?" or "Hey, I've got two tickets to *Scooby on Ice*, would you like to go next Saturday?"

Don't ask her when a bunch of people are around – This is more for your protection than hers. If she says no, you will have saved yourself a lot of embarrassment by not asking her in front of the entire class.

If she says no, don't ask why – Just say, "Okay, maybe another time," and walk away. If she wants to go out with you, she will give you another date that works, or she may just start flirting with you more.

Never ask her more than twice – If she says no 2 times in a row, she probably means no forever, unless she also tells you that she would "love to but can't this weekend, so how about next weekend?" You don't want to be a pest, but you also need to make sure she isn't just really busy. That is always a possibility.

Ask her yourself – Don't ask your friend to find out if she will date you. You gotta be a man someday, so why not today? Ask for yourself; don't be a middle schooler and find out if it's safe or not. Be a man!

Ask her out for one date at a time – Don't get all greedy and ask her out for several dates at once. Girls like a bit of mystery. When you are all over her too soon, it's a real turn-off.

Be direct – Say, "Would you like to . . . ?" Avoid things like, "I know you are busy, but I was wondering if maybe one day you . . ." Get to the point and get to it fast. Don't be a wimp. Be direct and know what you want.

Well, if you scored a date with Miss Perfect and want some info on what she's hoping for out of the deal, feast your eyes on these pages. We've got all you need to know about the big date from a girl's perspective. **What she likes**, wants, and, well, uh, needs. So dive into the wonderful world of dating. Bon voyage!

How to Be the Best Date Ever

Where to go. Remember, a date is a time for you 2 to talk. Girls love that! So don't take her to a movie or monster cars. Take her someplace where you guys can talk and get to know each other.

Info. Let her know ahead of time how she should dress so she won't be in high heels and a dress for your hike around the lake.

Plan the date. Girls love it when it looks like you've spent time planning something for them. Make plans. They don't have to cost you anything. Just get a plan of some kind. (Check out "the creative date" if you are out of ideas.)

Be on time. If you have to leave mega early, then do it. Just don't get to her house late.

Doorman. Get all doors for her—the car door, the restaurant door. Get them all and let her go through first, unless it's a revolving door, and then you go through first so you can push it.

It's all about her. Have everything the way she likes it. Ask her what kind of music she likes and play that. Don't have your fave garage punk band playing on high when you start the car.

Chair man. Pull out the chair for her and slowly push it in as she sits down. Then you can sit down.

Standing man. Stand up whenever she gets up from the table, enters the room, or leaves the room.

Ask her questions. Girls bond by talking. The more they can talk to you, the more they will like you. So make conversation. Talk with them, not at them.

Coat man. When she is putting on her coat, lift it up by the back of it and help her into it.

Seating. At the movies or theater, let her walk into the row of seats before you.

Pay. If you asked her, then you pay. No splitting the check.

Anticipation. At the end of a date, don't ask for another one. Save that for the next time you talk.

Best seat in the house. When you go out to eat give her the best seat. The woman should always have her back to the wall. That assures she has the best view. It will make you a gracious provider, and she will appreciate it.

more

hint Experts say that girls need to speak at least 30,000 words per day but guys only need to use 15,000 words per day.

Ask her as many questions about herself as you can. Make it a game. See how much info you can find out about her. Don't be a jerk and probe where she doesn't want you to, but get her talking about herself, her pets, her family, and anything else that she likes to talk about.

If you do all the talking and spend all your time trying to prove to her what a great guy you are, she is going to lose interest. She will think you don't care about her and only think about yourself. I know you are just trying to prove to her what a great catch you are, but for her the best catch is the one who listens to her and wants to know what makes her tick.

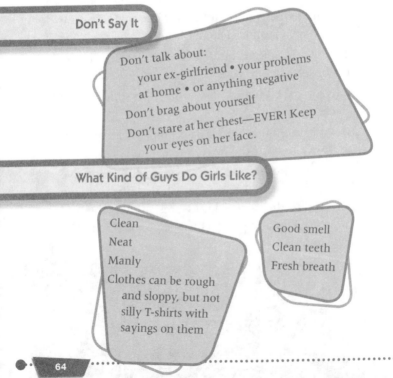

Don't Say It

Don't talk about:
your ex-girlfriend • your problems at home • or anything negative
Don't brag about yourself
Don't stare at her chest—EVER! Keep your eyes on her face.

What Kind of Guys Do Girls Like?

Clean
Neat
Manly
Clothes can be rough and sloppy, but not silly T-shirts with sayings on them

Good smell
Clean teeth
Fresh breath

Ideas for Date Conversation

Nothing's worse than sitting at dinner or some other place where all there is to do is talk and having nothing to say to each other. Talking is the meter the girl uses to figure out how the date is going. Silence can be death to her, so if talking to a girl isn't your forté, no fear. I've got a few pointers that will help you start a convo that makes her feel divine. So here's the 411 on making your date feel comfortable with you from start to finish.

- Ask her lots of questions about herself. Make them "how," "why," and "when" questions so she has to say more than yes and no back to ya.

> Where did you grow up?
> How many brothers and sisters do you have?
> Do you have any pets? What are their names?
> What is your favorite class?
> What do you do on weekends?
> What are your favorite TV shows, sports teams, etc.?

- Talk about your favorite hobby and why you like it, but then be sure to ask her what she thinks and what her fave hobby is.

- Compliment something about her, then ask her a question about it.

> "I love your hair. Do you get a lot of compliments on it?"
> "I love your jeans. Where did you get them?"

- Find out about her spirit. Ask her questions about her faith and her relationship with God.

- Talk about the food. If you are eating together, always ask her how she likes the food. Find out what she likes best about it. Ask her about her favorite food in the world. If she could only eat one thing for the rest of her life, what would it be?

- Ask her about her future. Talk about what you want to do and find out what she dreams of doing.

- Give and take is the key. Ask her a question, listen, then talk a little about the same subject, then ask more questions. Keep the conversation going like a volley-ball going back and forth over the net.

Make Her Smile

How do you make the girl of your dreams smile? Try this.

Call her just to talk

Tell her how cute she is

Bring her a stuffed animal when she is sick

Write her a poem

Look into her eyes

Go shopping with her and pay attention to what she is looking at

Ask her out

Tell her 5 reasons why you like her

Write her a little note and slip it in her locker or book

Send her a card in the mail

Pay attention when she is talking

Slow dance with her

Carry her books

Get the door for her

Remember things she has told you

True romance is doing something for the other person just because you care, not in order to get something back.

Here are some Different Date Ideas that will help you to look like a great catch.

Photo Shoot – Buy 2 disposable cameras and go somewhere like a train yard, flower farm, zoo, or any other funky place around town, and then shoot 24 pics. Make it into an art project. Then plan a time to get back together and look over your pics. (Note: You should take both cameras and develop them both. If you don't want a 2nd date, let her take the camera she used and develop the pics herself.)

Scavenger Hunt – Make her go on a scavenger hunt. Give her a note that tells her where she needs to go first. Make it a fun place that she might like—like give her $20 in an envelope and tell her to go to the Gap and buy herself something small. Or send her to the flower shop to pick up some flowers that you have already paid for. When she gets to the first location, have another note there for her that will lead her to another place. Give her about 4 places to go before she gets to where you are.

Explore – Go somewhere neither of you has gone before.

Teach – Teach your date something that you do really well.

Taste Testing – Pick one kind of food or drink that she loves, like hot chocolate or apple pie, then go to 4 restaurants and judge each one based on the quality and taste. Talk about the food you choose to judge, the special tastes, the way it's served, the service. Make a night of being a food critic.

Q&A – Get a book of questions and spend the evening over dinner asking each other weird stuff that you never would have thought of.

Theme Date – Find out what your date likes and build the date around that. If she loves Italy, make it an Italian night. Bring her Italian chocolate, take her to an Italian resto, buy an Italian CD to play in the car, and then rent an Italian movie with subtitles.

Vacation at Home – Never been a tourist in your own town? Well, give it a try. Go to the local visitors' bureau (or chamber of commerce) and ask about touristy things to do in your area. The staff there can help you come up with all kinds of fun things to do. You can even decide to take a camera around with you and ask people to take pictures of you guys. Girls love memory-makers like photos.

Group Date – Don't just do the usual movie or mall trip, but plan a dinner. Invite a group over to a fancy dinner with dresses and suits. Or make it a theme party, ala Italy or BBQ. Have everyone bring something that relates to the theme.

Backwards Dinner – Have dinner backwards! Start with dessert and work your way back.

Other
Not-So-Different-But-Still-a-Date
Date Ideas

Water park or amusement park

Bowling

Roller blading

Hiking

Picnic in the park

Museum or art gallery

Old folks home (talk to the old people, find out about their pasts, help them out)

Dance class

Pottery painting

Rock climbing gym

Canoeing or boating

Play horseshoes

Walk on the beach with your shoes off, or sit on the boardwalk and talk

Golfing

Bike tour

Girls You Shouldn't Date

Don't date a girl just because of her reputation.

Don't date a girl who pressures you to be more like a girl.

Don't date your best friend's ex.

Don't date a girl who has a different faith than yours.

Don't date girls who use their emotions to manipulate people.

Are You More Than Friends?

How to know if she "likes you, likes you"
or just wants to be friends

Sometimes girls just want to hang out with you and
not necessarily date you. But figuring this out can be
difficult unless you know the telltale clues:

Physicalness – If you have been on a few dates and
there has been no hint of any kind of physical
affection, this might be just a friendship.

Conversation topics – If you never talk about
intimate stuff like feelings, hopes, and dreams,
then your relationship might not be that kind
of a relationship.

Her friends – If her friends all say things like, "You
guys are such great friends," or are talking about
your date's other relationships, you're probably
just friends.

The rumor mill – If rumor has it that she is seeing other people, chances are you guys are just
friends.

HOW TO BE THE PERFECT BOYFRIEND

Mr. Perfect
—The Short List—

'd like to tell you I have some sort of master list that you can simply follow step by step to become Mr. Perfect to any girl you want. Keep on dreamin'! I can't help you there, but I can help you with a couple of things that most girls want in a guy. Don't worry if you aren't Rico Suave at all these things; if you just know about them and try to practice them you will be way ahead of most guys.

Be Confident

Confidence isn't something that we all have. And you might wonder how to get it if you don't have it naturally. Let me give you a secret: confidence has less to do with what you think about yourself and more to do with what you think about others. The key to looking confident is caring about other people, and by that I mean all people, not just your date. Talk to people, smile at them, and realize how valuable they all are. When you care for people, girls realize that you are a good guy. When a guy is really nice to a waiter and gets to know his name and talks with him more like a person than a servant, something inside the girl goes "ca-ching!" and she adds another point to your love bank account. You get good points for appearing confident by caring for people who can't do anything to get you what you want in life. So care about people and you will look confident. How do you do that? Here are some quick tips:

✔ Talk to people in line with you. Make polite convo.

✔ Tip people who are in the service industry. You might not be rich, but you have enough to give a guy a buck for helping you out with something.

✔ Help other women get doors and carry things. When you care about all people, your girl digs it. But remember, she is always first on your list. Don't run off to help someone and leave her hanging.

✔ Don't yell at people when you drive.

✔ Don't be afraid to talk to anyone—old people, young people, talk to them all.

Communicate

Now, I'm not asking you to get all girly on me and get in touch with your feminine side, heaven forbid. I want you to be a guy through and through, but I also want you to understand how you can meet the needs of the girl you are dating. I want you to be prepared to treat her the way she was made to be treated, and that means you have to learn a little bit about communication. It's the biggest, most important thing for girls. They live for it. They love it. They are all about the talking. I know, I know, shut up already, you want to say. And I don't blame you, but the fact of the matter is, they are never going to totally shut up, and you don't want them to, 'cuz when they talk, they fall in love. No talking, no falling in love. So what's the deal with communicating with girls? How can you do it so you are still a guy but also a girl magnet? Here are a few things you need to know about how girls operate. Try some of them out and see if they don't work for you.

✔ After a date, call her. There are 2 things you need to know about calling. Number 1, it's normal in girl world to call each other after doing something just to talk about it and confirm that it was really great. So if it was your 1st date, call her somewhere between the next day and 4 days after the date. Tell her how great it was. Talk about some of the stuff you did and why you liked it. And number 2, the call is a good time to ask her out again. If you have been going out for a while, it's really cool to call her whenever you want—even as soon as you get home—just to tell her you had a great time. Say, "You know what I liked best about tonight?" and then tell her one thing about her that you loved. Let her talk about the date and communicate how she feels.

✔ If you guys are steady and you call her regularly, then it's a good idea to tell her what you like about her. You *should* do this every day, but occasionally go the extra mile and give her a list of like 5 things about her that you love. Let her tell you what she likes about you if she wants to.

✔ Ask her questions. The key to communicating with a girl is letting her talk. And the best way for her to talk is to talk about good things. Don't let her get caught up in telling you all her miseries; rehearsing all the crap in her life only makes her more depressed. Ask her stuff like, "If you could go anywhere in the world, where would it be?" or "If money were no object and you could do whatever you want for the rest of your life, what would it be?" Find a book of questions and pull it out for an occasional chat session.

✔ Send her an email or card for no reason.

✔ Give her a little gift. Girls don't need big fancy gifts to feel loved; they just need a gift. It can be a pack of Life Savers and a note. Just make sure that you give her stuff. It doesn't have to be every day, but occasionally a gift is a major point-maker for you. It communicates that you like her and are thinking about her.

✔ Compliment her. Remember, compliments communicate a lot to a girl. Be sure to notice how nice her hair is, or her nails, or her clothes. Notice it.

✔ Look her in the eye when she talks. When she is telling you something, don't look around the room. Don't watch TV or get distracted by stuff going on around you. To girls if you aren't looking them in the eyes, that means you aren't listening. So keep your eyes on her.

✔ Sympathize with her. When she is bummed or angry about something, don't try to correct her or fix the problem. Just tell her how bad you feel for her and let her vent on you. The best thing you can do for a girl is sympathize with her feelings, not try to change them.

✔ Bring her flowers. This gift is often overlooked by guys, but flowers don't have to be expensive to score major points with girls. If you don't have much cash, stop by a vacant lot and pick wildflowers. Wrap them in newspaper and a bow. She'll love the effort. Roses are kinda serious, so save those for the proposal. Find other kinds of flowers like tulips, daisies, or whatever's unique and fits her personality. Get creative.

Make her a mix CD. Put all her fave songs on it, ones that you can listen to on your next date. She'll keep it forever.

definition **sympathy:**
the act or capacity of entering into or sharing the feelings or interests of another. Also something that girls really dig.

Having a Girlfriend:

How to Date Someone
More Than Once

When you have a girlfriend, it's important to know how to take care of her—that is, if you want to keep her. And don't get all caveman on me; what I'm talking about isn't becoming some kind of a girly-man. What I'm talking about is learning to genuinely love someone other than yourself. Listen, guys, as believers in Christ we have a different set of rules. We are called to love one another, our friends, our families, and even our enemies, so how much more the girl of your dreams? Remember, love isn't about getting something; it's about giving. Christ is the perfect example of love. Check him out—what did he do for those he loves? He gave. He gave and he gave. He gave it all. And he never once complained about it. So the first thing you have to do in learning to have a girlfriend (or eventually a wife even) is learn to love. (For more on this, read *Defining True Love*, page 117.) And part of loving is giving people what they need that you have. Girls need different things than guys do, duh, but what that is isn't always so obvious. But you're smart enough to know that if you figure out what they need, it's a heck of a lot easier to make them happy and so to create a great relationship. So check out this list of guy jobs when it comes to taking care of your woman.

The DTR – Define the Relationship

It's crucial for the *guy* to define the relationship. It's part of leadership. Girls continually want to know where they stand with you, and as a guy, it's your job to tell them. Not that you have to tell her every day, but as the relationship progresses, it's very cool for you to tell her. If you've been dating other people and you decide you only want to date her, let her know. Define the relationship as exclusive. If you've gotten exclusive and you want to move toward marriage, then let her know. Define the relationship. Don't make the girl do the asking. *"What am I to you?" "Where do you see us in 2 years?"*

If you wanna be a guy your girl adores, then tell her how you feel so she doesn't have to ask. Tell her what you want her to be in your life. Make her feel special, and she will adore you even more.

PMS – How to Deal When She Can't Deal

Okay, if you date a girl for any length of time, you are bound to run into the dreaded PMS. That's the time right before her period (it can be between 2 and 10 days before) when she is very emotional. You've probably been on the receiving end of bad PMS, but what the heck makes her so crazy? It's hormones. When her body goes through this time of the month, her hormones get all out of whack. I know this subject is gross to you, but if you want to date girls, you'd better learn more about them, or you'll be miserable the rest of your life.

What does it feel like to have PMS? I know that you as a guy, will never truly understand, but let me see if I can't help you start to get the picture of what it feels like to have PMS. Just to be clinical, here are some of the symptoms:

- Irritability
- Frustration
- Bloating
- Mood swings
- Food cravings
- Depression
- Exhaustion
- Anger
- Panic
- Backaches
- Fatigue
- Breast swelling and tenderness
- Headaches

Gee, doesn't that sound like a fun list to experience every month? Well, that's what girls are up against. Some girls have it worse than others, but most of us will have to deal with at least a few of these things throughout our lives.

When a girl has PMS she can feel crazy—literally like she is going crazy. Sometimes she has virtually no control of her emotions; they just take her wherever they want, and usually it's not to a good place. Since anger is one symptom of PMS, you never know what she might get mad about.

So how do you deal with this crazy woman? Here's a list of pointers to help you through this time of the month:

- Never, I repeat, *never* ask her if she is "on the rag." Bad, bad, bad. That just means you think she's being a brat and you want her to stop. She might be mad, but she can still see through your jerkiness. If you really want to know if she has PMS so you can know how to handle her actions, then try something more caring, like, "Boy, it sure seems like you feel awful right now. Do you know any reason why you might be feeling like this?" If she isn't sure, then you can ask her if it might be PMS. That might help her out because sometimes, believe it or not, we have no idea why we feel so bad. We forget the time of the month and don't realize what's happening to us. Remembering can help us know we aren't crazy or in need of a major life change.

- Don't take what she says as her final thoughts on a matter, especially when she's mad. The best policy for a girl with PMS is to make no major decisions, because she isn't sure what she really thinks or feels. So if she gets mad at you and wants to break up or pick a fight, try to take it lightly. Don't get caught up in her PMS. Give her space if she's acting crazy, or rub her back if that would help her feel better. This isn't a sexual advance; it's a pain-relieving one. Take care of her and in the end, she'll get better and take care of you.

Know that it *will* end. Generally as soon as she starts her period, her hormones will get back to normal and she'll be fine. So just hold on.

No caffeine or sugar. You don't have much control over your girl, but if you can, try not to feed her caffeine or sugar for 10 days before her period. If she avoids that stuff she'll feel better and not get so angry. So don't push her to eat it.

Don't start any fights or ask any major decision–type questions during PMS. If you can figure out her schedule you'll be better off, 'cuz you never want to pick a fight when she has PMS. It's sure to turn into more than you bargained for, so avoid it. Just be nice!

Communicating with a Girlfriend

A girlfriend is a serious thing. She requires lots of attention and work. Yeah, the payoff can be amazing, but back to the work. It's not an easy ride having a girlfriend. Girls are different from guys in so many ways, and unless you really get them you can totally fail as a boyfriend. So here's some stuff you need to know about keeping things alive with your girlfriend.

Calling

Girls love to talk, in case you hadn't noticed. And talking on the phone is one of the dreamiest things we can do. So if you have a gf, then boy, it's time to let your fingers do the walking, and I don't mean on your girlfriend, stupid! I mean on the phone. Girls love phone calls, so make sure that you call her regularly. You'll figure out from her how much is the right amount. Each girl is different. But whatever you do, make sure you call her at least a couple times a week. The key is that the more you call her, the more she thinks you love her. It goes kinda like this:

Call her once a week – She thinks you could be interested but is also probably telling her friends you are such a jerk for not calling. This isn't so bad if you don't really want to get too close to her, but if you want a serious relationship, you need to up the call quotient.

Call her 2–3 times a week – She's starting to feel better. She still thinks you are kind of a schmuck because you can't seem to commit, but if you are nice to her and talk a long time when you do call, she will forget all about that and just hope for more.

Call her 4–6 times a week – She's all yours. You'll have a secure girlfriend who is glad that the relationship is getting stronger. She'll feel really good about her place in your life, though she will still dream of a time when you'll call every day.

Call her every day – You are a serious item. She's already thinking about the wedding and what to name the kids. You are her dream man. Remember, the more you talk, the more she bonds, which means the more she likes you and the more she thinks you like her.

Your Schedule

If you have a serious girlfriend, be prepared, because your time is no longer your own. For most girls your weekends are all about her. She wants you 2 to be together. This can be a blast if your gf is into the same stuff as you. So if you want to keep this great catch, make sure that you talk about the weekend sometime during the week so she knows what you guys will be doing together and separately. A lot of girls expect that since you are dating, you will spend all weekend together. But just because that's what they think doesn't necessarily mean that's what should happen. Here are some pointers on managing your schedule while you are dating someone.

Your Friends

Having a girlfriend doesn't mean you can't spend some weekend time with your boys, but if she doesn't have stuff to keep herself busy then beware, 'cuz she won't be liking the fact that she's all alone while you are with your friends. She could start clinging to you more and more if you are her only social life. You aren't being faithful to her or to God if you allow yourself to become her all in all. So make sure she understands why you are doing your own thing. Help her to understand that it's good for both of you to have things to do separately. Make sure she knows that it isn't about not wanting to be with her; it's about wanting to be healthy and both of you to keep your other friendships alive.

Your Families

Once you start dating it's really easy to start to do things with each other's families, but watch out—the more you bring a family into your relationship, the harder it will be when it ends. You won't be breaking up with just the girl but with the whole fam. The best thing to do is to get to know her family but not become a *part* of the family. If you aren't married to her, don't act like you are. Save the son-in-law stuff for marriage, or it will really feel like a divorce when it's over.

Honoring Her Parents

Honoring her parents has 3 bonuses:

1. If she is a smart girl, she will totally dig that you want to honor her parents.
2. If her parents like you and trust you, your dating life will be much better. If they don't trust you, they just might cramp your style.
3. God is kinda big on this subject. It's all about the honor: "Honor your father and your mother, that your days may be long in the land that the LORD your God is giving you" (Exodus 20:12 ESV).

So how do you do it?

1. Find out the rules. This sounds freaky, but it will help you grow on the man-scale by 100 percent.

Tell her 'rents that you want to honor them, and ask them what rules they have for dating their daughter. Find out what her curfew is, where you can take her, etc.

2. Let them know that you want to protect her, then explain how you will do that. In case you are clueless, here's a good place to start:

a. You will never be alone with her in a bedroom or a house. (Do I need to tell you why? I hope so. I hope this comes as a total shock to you: being alone with your gf is the first step to sexual activity. Want to avoid the drama? Then avoid the being alone. It makes fooling around just too dang easy.)

b. You will protect her wherever you go. Let them know—and you'd better mean it—that you won't drive too fast when she is in the car with you. You will be careful and make sure she doesn't get hurt. That's part of being the man too—taking care of the girl.

As long as her parents pay for her food, clothing, and shelter, she has to live by their rules! So when it comes to dating, you'd better find out what those rules are and live by them. She might push you to break a rule here and there, but don't let her be the guy, leading you along like some wimp. Be strong. Be the man. Let her know that you intend to obey her parents' rules and that's that. And remind her of her responsibility in God's eyes to honor them as well.

The Big M Word: Marriage

Okay, I'm going to let you in on a big secret here (if you haven't read *Dateable*, then this will be news to you): most of us girls are already planning the wedding and naming the babies once we start crushing on you. It's true. Why else would we practice signing our first name with your last name? We're getting ready for the big day! So think about that next time you tell her you will "love her forever" or something mushy like that. Don't play with her emotions and lead her on. You might not be trying to, but sometimes she misreads what you say. So try to be really sensitive to her marriage fantasies, and don't feed them unless you plan on marrying her in the next year. If it's longer than that then don't lead her on. You never know how things might change over time.

The Best Boyfriend on Earth

To make her feel like the most important person in your life . . .

Compliment her

Put her first

Invite her to things

Think of her before you commit to do stuff

Find out what she is feeling

Let her talk with you about her feelings

Tell her often how important she is to you

Tell her things like, "I noticed you the first time I saw you and have wanted to get to know you ever since."

Don't act like her problems are stupid or silly. If she is worried about something, be on her side. Sympathize with her. Tell her how awful she must feel and how unfair that is. Be her ally; don't correct her.

The Dateable Rules

for Guys

1. **Being a Guy Is Good** – *Dateable* guys know that they aren't as sensitive as girls and that's okay. They know that they are stronger, more dangerous, and more adventurous and that's okay too. *Dateable* guys are real men who aren't afraid to be guys.

2. **Believe in Yourself** – *Dateable* guys know they are men even if someone has tried to bring them down or make them less than men. They know that the past doesn't define the future.

3. **Control Your Mind** – *Dateable* guys know that God demands self-control. They learn ways to control their minds so they can control their bodies.

4. **Don't Just Want a Win, Want an Adventure** – *Dateable* guys know life is about danger. You might not win, but that's not the point—*doing* it is. *Dateable* guys risk failure to live the adventure of life.

5. **Face Your Fears** – *Dateable* guys will not be controlled by fear. Whatever controls you, owns you. Fear is from the enemy, so the *Dateable* guy stands in the face of it and says, "Bring it on!"

6. **Men of God Are Wild, Not Domesticated** – *Dateable* guys aren't tamed. They don't live by the same rules as the opposite sex. They fight battles, conquer lands, and stand up for the oppressed.

7. **Read God into It** – *Dateable* guys read God into it. They ask, "What would he say if he could talk to me through this situation?"

8. **Be Honest with Girls** – *Dateable* guys don't use the truth to their advantage. They know that girls read into things, so they don't use that for their good. They are honest and not manipulative.

9. **Be a Gentleman** – Chivalry is not dead with the *Dateable* guy. Even if society thinks this is old-fashioned, he knows that it is God-fashioned. He keeps his gentleman's side strong and considers all women important enough to care for.

10. **Keep It Covered Up** – *Dateable* guys know that porn is bad for the spirit and the mind. They keep women covered up.

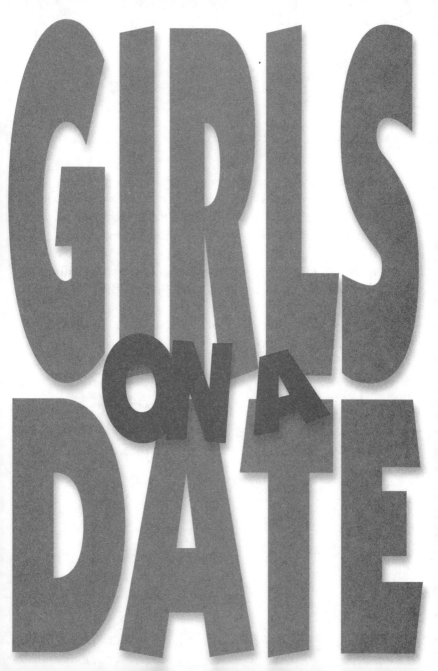

Be His Best Date Ever

The thing to remember on a date with a guy is that, uh, well, he is the guy. Seems obvious, I know, but it really isn't as easy as it sounds. On a date your job is not to be in charge. It is not to control the conversation, the stuff you do, or the time it takes to do it. Your job is to like his ideas of things to do and to be fun to be with, kind, and caring. Remember, you aren't out with your best girlfriend, so it isn't a crab session or a tell-me-your-life-history event. It's a chance for him to see if you are worth the chase. It's a dance. You follow, he leads.

Taboo Topics for the First Date

Don't talk about . . .
- your ex-boyfriend(s)
- your problems at home
- your pet's antics
- anything negative
- your health problems
- how much you want to get married
- how much you like him
- how great you are

1. Don't offer to meet him somewhere. Let him come get you. He loves that part.

2. Slow down and let him get doors. That's him showing you that he is a gentleman, so don't try to steal that job from him. (Note: If it's a revolving door, let him go in first so he can push it.)

3. Don't reach across and unlock his door. If you were considered important enough to have your door opened, then you shouldn't then have to reach across and unlock his side, especially if you are nicely dressed. Some guys might think that is unkind of you, but deep down when you *do* reach across they know that their service to you of opening your door isn't as special.

4. At the movies or theater, once you together pick the best place, go into the row of seats first.

5. Talk about good things. Don't whine about bad stuff.

6. Laugh at his jokes (or his attempts at jokes).

7. If he is talking too much, don't ask him a lot of questions. He doesn't bond by talking like you do, so if you think that asking him questions makes him like you more, you are wrong. It just makes him like himself more. Let him ask *you* questions, and if he doesn't then feel free to just interrupt him to make comments on what he is saying. Guys interrupt each other; that's how they talk. They don't ask questions. So feel free to be part of the convo and cut in. Don't change the subject; just join in.

8. Let him pay, and then say, "Thank you for dinner. That was so nice of you. I loved it." This is a big part of letting him lead. It is a symbol of him as provider and protector. (Note: If you go out with this guy a lot, you can start to offer to pay every so often. But not all the time, and definitely not on the first date.)

9. Let him plan the date. Some guys have no idea how to do this, but they should. If he asks, he plans. If he doesn't plan, then you can make a suggestion, but don't take that role away from him if he is man enough to step into it.

10. Let him get your chair. A true gentleman will pull out your chair for you and slowly push it in as you sit down. Smile and say thank you.

11. Eat. Order a sensible meal, meaning one you can eat. And then eat it. Don't order a steak and then not touch it—oooh, he hates that—or a small salad and water. You eat, so don't pretend you don't. Guys love to see a girl with a good appetite. It's one of the things they find attractive in girls.

12. Make conversation, but if he is really nervous and talks about himself the entire time, don't get upset. That's just his way of telling you how much of a catch he is and how much he wants to prove to you that he's worthy of you. By the second date he should be more calm and open to hearing from you.

13. Don't call him the next day or even the next week. Let him call you. You are the one who is being chased, not the chaser. Call him first and I guarantee you'll drop 5 points on the hotness scale.

Always say thank you.

Talking on the Phone with Boys

Several phases are involved in talking on the phone with boys.

Phase 1 – In the beginning of the relationship, you want to let the guy chase you. That doesn't mean play too hard to get; it just means that the harder you are to get, the more he will like you. So it goes like this: if he is just starting to show an interest in you, the last thing he needs is the marathon conversation. I know, for you it's a bonding moment, but for him it's too long for a conversation to go. So if you want to really get him to like you and want to call you back again, keep it short. Talk 15–20 minutes max. If he is still talking after that long, tell him you really have to go but thanks for calling.

This way when he gets off the phone he isn't saying, "Sheesh, that girl can talk." He's saying, "Wow, I really like her. I can't wait to talk to her again." So try to keep it short in the beginning of the relationship.

Phase 2 – This starts when you've been on a few dates. You are starting to feel more comfortable with each other, and he's starting to call more often. This is when you get to find out a lot about each other and start to become friends. I still recommend keeping the convos short, but you can ramp 'em up to 30 minutes to 1 hour. But don't go over that, or you run the risk of giving just too much info. Remember, guys are hunters. Don't be like the deer who just walks out and goes, "Here I am, shoot me." That's no fun at all. Don't hang on the phone too long and he'll be dying to call you back.

Phase 3 – In phase three you are an item. You've been going out for quite a while, and you spend a lot of time together. You might even call yourselves best friends. If he is really wanting to talk and still calling you a lot, then you can ramp up your convos based on how much you think he is enjoying them. If you are the only one talking most of the time, he is probably not having the best time of his life, so take it easy on the guy. Spend some of that talking energy on your girlfriends. They were made for it; he wasn't.

> **hint**
>
> Silence doesn't have to be filled. If he is quiet, it isn't always because he is mad or upset. Don't always try to fill up the silence.

Don't date . . .

guys with different religious beliefs than you

a guy just because your parents don't like him

a guy just because it will make you more popular

a guy who has a rep for being a user

your best friend's ex

anyone who is more than 2 years older than you until you are over 21

someone just because you were afraid to say no when they asked you out

a guy who has already gotten a girl pregnant

a guy who makes you feel ugly

a guy who cuts you down, even if he says he's sorry

a guy who tries to control you with words or violence

7 Questions

You Should Never Ask a Guy

1. **What are you thinking?** Never ask a guy this. It isn't any of your business what another person is thinking, and besides, it's probably not anything you want him to be thinking. Just avoid the subject.

2. **Do you think _____ is cute?** Danger! Don't try to be his buddy. You are his girlfriend. You put him in a really bad position when you start to talk about other girls with him. Nothing good will come out of this, so avoid the subject of other girls' cuteness.

3. **Can we talk about defining the relationship?** Don't ever ask a guy to *define the relationship*. Too much pressure. It's like those used car salesmen who say, "What will it take to get you to buy this car today?" It's just ugly. It's unflattering and insecure. If he has any intentions for continuing the relationship, you won't have to ask. He'll be eager to not lose you. And if he is the man, he will be the one leading the relationship and therefore defining it. Leaders define—that's how they tell you where they are leading you so that you will follow.

4. **Do you like hanging out with the guys more than with me?** No, no. Don't ask what you might not like to hear. It's not fair to ask a guy this. That's like him asking if you like him more than shopping. Tough choice, huh? Again, quit prying into the psyche of your guy; it isn't your domain. He has a right to his private thoughts, and when you try to barge into them, you only make him think less of you. And besides, every time you ask him something like this, you run the risk of driving him to lie to you. He's trapped, because even if he loves his guy friends, he has to tell you no, he likes hanging out with you more.

That's something that he won't feel good about, and now he's tainted the relationship with a little lie.

5. **Who just called?** When his cell rings you don't have a right to ask him who it is. Stop trying to control him by controlling information. Let him have his privacy and his life. He's not your husband. And asking only makes him uncomfortable.

6. **Where were you last night?** Sounds more like an accusation than curiosity. If he wants to tell you where he was, he will tell you. But when you start giving him the 3rd degree, you lose your mystery. Keep the mystery alive and let him have his life. Trust, that's the key ingredient. When you trust someone they want to live up to that trust. So no asking them leading questions.

7. **Why don't you call me more often?** Anything that begins with "why don't you" is an immediate no-no. You put him on the defensive with this kind of accusation. It says to him that he isn't good enough for you. He isn't meeting your needs. If you want to talk about this, change it to a statement: "I really love it when you call. It's fun talking to you on the phone." Positive reinforcement gets you what you want better than a negative question.

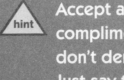

Accept a compliment, don't deny it. Just say thank you.

Do You Like Me, Like Me?

Sometimes guys just want to hang out with you a lot but not necessarily date you. Figuring this out can be difficult unless you know the telltale clues:

Physicalness – If you have been on a few dates and there has been no hint of any kind of physical affection—touching your hair or your arm, offering you his arm as you walk, holding hands, etc.—then this might just be a friendship.

Sweet talk – If he never says anything sweet like "I love your eyes" or "You smell so good," then your relationship might not be *that* kind of a relationship.

His friends – If his friends all say things like, "You guys are such great friends" or are talking about your guy's other relationships, that's kinda a no-brainer. You're just buds, period, the end.

The rumor mill – If rumor has it that your crush is seeing other people, chances are you guys are just friends.

So what do you do if you've come to the conclusion that it's Friendsville for you 2? I'm not going to pretend I fully understand your guy or the relationship you 2 have, but as an objective observer I can say that if he's just friending it with you and you "like him, like him," it's time to cut ties. You can't keep on killing yourself, leading yourself on with hopes of him changing his feelings. It just isn't going to happen—at least not while you keep giving him his cake while he's eating it too with some other girl. If there's any hope at all for your guy to see how much he truly loves you, it is when you aren't around. If he misses you, he might start to think more highly of you and rethink your relationship. But until then, stop seeing him, because it's not healthy pining after someone who doesn't love you. And don't put all your eggs in the "he'll-miss-me-too-much-and-want-me-for-his-girlfriend" basket. That might happen or it might never happen. The point is that you need to move on. Get honest with yourself and stop the lies.

HOW TO BE THE PERFECT GIRLFRIEND

Having a

When you have a boyfriend, it's important to know how to take care of him—that is, if you want to keep him. And don't get all Gloria Steinem on me; what I'm talking about isn't being his servant but loving him and caring about how he feels. After all, as believers in Christ we have a different set of rules. We are called to love one another, our friends, our families, and even our enemies, so how much more the guy of your dreams? Remember, love isn't about getting something; it's about giving. Christ is the perfect example of love. Check him out—what did he do for those he loves? He gave. He gave and he gave. He gave it all. And he never once complained about it. So the first thing you have to do in learning to have a boyfriend (and eventually a husband) is learn to love. (For more on this, read *Defining True Love*, page 117.) And part of loving is giving people what they need that you have. Guys need different things than us girls do, but what isn't always obvious. If you know what they need, it's a heck of a lot easier to make them happy and so to create a great relationship. So check out this list.

How to Be the Best Girlfriend Ever

Be his biggest fan. You should be your boyfriend's biggest fan. Never, ever, I mean *ever* join in with others

Boyfriend:

when they cut him down, slam him, or criticize him in any way. And never, ever, ever start the games yourself by telling others anything bad about your guy. If you are dating someone, you need to build trust, and guys need to know that you've got their back. If you want to lose his trust and destroy his pride all at once, then make fun of him in front of other people. It will be a major blow. But if you want to really make him happy, stand up for him. Be his biggest fan.

Appreciate the stuff he does. Comment on what he does, not who he is. Guys are all about accomplishment. If you can tell him what a good job he did at picking out the movie, choosing the restaurant, or catching the game-winning pass, then do it. You get major points when you appreciate him for what he does.

Ask him for help on something. When you ask a guy for help, you allow him to shine. Guys love to show you what they can do. Sure, it might be showing off, but they show off to get your attention. So let them show off. Let them show you how they can change your oil, move something heavy, or fix your stereo.

Agree with him. When a guy tells you what he thinks about something, agree with him. If you think he's totally off his rocker, you can feel free to argue, but when you agree, let him know. He loves to be proved right. And if he is giving you advice, tell him, "I had never thought of it like that. I have another way of thinking of it." So even if you think he's whacked out, you can still help him save face by telling him the value of what he said before you show him why you're right. It's called being gracious. It isn't stupid or silly for a girl to be gracious and kind to someone before presenting her argument (check out Proverbs 18:13).

Give him guy time. When you let a guy have time to be with the guys without whining about it, you score major points. Don't think that just because you are dating suddenly he's all yours. That's not only stupid, it's dysfunctional. You both need to keep your friends and do things without each other. If you don't, then you aren't a friend anybody would want, so don't expect your friends to be there when you need 'em.

Know how to get what you want. If your guy isn't all you want him to be, don't panic. There is hope. I know your first instinct is to start complaining, hoping that will fix the problem. "You don't call me enough." "How come you spend so much time with your guy friends?" But the second you start to accuse him of anything, he shuts down. I mean, who would want to be nice to someone who just slugged you in the stomach? And that's what a negative question is to a guy—it's a total cut-down.

It's like this. If he said he'd be to your house at 7:00 and he doesn't get there till 7:30, your first instinct is to yell at him. I mean, he's always late. He really needs to learn to be on time. But the way he sees it, the first thing he hears from you when he comes to pick you up is you yelling at him about always being late. So tell me, do you think that makes him say to himself, "Boy, I really love it when I pick her up. I love the accusations and the attacks. I think I'll come earlier next time so she can start sooner"? I don't think so! The key to helping guys change is positive reinforcement. Tell them what you like, not what you don't like. When they do something good, reward them. If he calls, don't say, "I can't believe you haven't called me in 2 days!" Instead try this: "Gosh, it's so nice to hear from you. I'm so glad you called." Now suddenly, just like a dog learning tricks, he thinks, "Call and get a treat. Call and she will love me more. Hmmm. Good idea to call more often." It's simple, really. Give people love for the good stuff they do and shut up about the stuff they forget to do. It's the best way to love someone and the best way to love yourself.

DDTR—*don't* define the relationship. It's crucial for the *guy* to define the relationship, not you! It's part of guy leadership. I know that you continually want to know where you stand with your guy, but you can't ask him. When you do ask him, two things happen. One is that you have just taken the lead, both from the guy and from God. Before you make a mistake and attempt to take your future into your hands, think about this: Do you trust God and his Word? Do you believe he wants you to have a godly man who you can feel good about allowing to lead you? Do you trust God to bring that man to you and to help him to be the leader he needs to be? If you answered yes to any of these, then **don't define the relationship.** Because when you do, you take the lead on your future and don't allow God or your man to lead you.

As if that isn't bad enough, the second thing that happens when you define the relationship is that most guys get totally freaked out. The chase that they so love is completely brought to a halt as you turn the tide and start to chase them. A lot of times guys will feel trapped and scared that you are too needy. Guys like to be needed, but they don't like it when you are too needy. When this happens all the mystery is gone. The excitement for him of hoping to one day catch you flies out the window and he quickly loses interest.

So do all you can to resist the temptation to take matters into your own hands. Don't define the relationship. And if things just get too slow and you can't stand the fact that the relationship isn't defined, then back off. Start dating other guys. The best way to find out his intentions is to slow down and see if he wants to speed back up again.

Being the best girlfriend on earth really has to do with controlling yourself. Don't jump into things and try to "fix" them just to get what you want when you want it. Think "delayed gratification." A woman of mystery trusts God with her love life and doesn't have to *manhandle* every situation that she thinks is going too slow for her. Think peace. Think patience. And let him take the lead. Remember, that's God's ultimate plan: the husband to be the head of the wife. And Christ to be the head of the man.

How to Be a Girl He'll Be Proud Of

Here is a list of qualities that will flip his lid. If you wanna know how to be his dream girl, then read on, wise one.

Be Confident

Confidence isn't something that we all have. And you might wonder how to get it if you don't have it naturally. Let me give you a secret: confidence has less to do with what you think about yourself and more to do with what you think about others. The key to looking confident is caring about other people, and by that I mean all people, not just your date. Talk to people, smile at them, and realize how valuable they all are. When you care for people guys realize that you are a good catch. When a girl is really nice to a waitress and gets to know her name and talks with her more like a person than a servant, something inside the guy goes "ca-ching!" and he adds another point to your love bank account. You get good points for caring for people who can't do anything to get you what you want in life. So care about people and you will look confident. So how do you do that? Here are some quick tips:

- Talk to people in line with you. Make polite convo.
- Tip people who are in the service industry. You might not be rich, but you have enough to give a guy a buck for helping you out with something.
- Help anyone older than you get doors and carry things. When you care about all people, he digs it. But remember, he is always first on your list. Don't run off to help someone and leave him hanging.
- Don't complain.
- Don't be afraid to talk to anyone—old people, young people, talk to them all.

Appreciate Him

One of the best things you can do for a guy is to appreciate him. Guys feel good when what they do gets noticed and appreciated by girls. Just like you like someone to notice how cute your dress is or how funky you do your hair all the time, guys like to be recognized for what they do. So after the movie, tell him how good the movie was and he'll feel great. After all, he picked it. But if you complain about the movie, it's like you're complaining about him. So try to find the good in stuff. Tell him thank you for all the stuff he does. When he gets the door, say thank you, and at the end of the date tell him thanks for the evening. Always say thank you for the things he does, and he will feel great.

The Best Girlfriend on Earth

Is there such a thing? Well, there might be if she looks something like this:

- She appreciates the things he does and tells him so.
- She doesn't complain.
- She's happy.
- She doesn't tell him all her problems all the time.
- She doesn't ask him what he's feeling.
- She lets him have his own interests, whether she likes them or not.
- She lets him have guy time.
- She doesn't smother him or act too needy.
- She lets him take the lead in things.

The Dateable Rules
for Girls

1. Accept Your Girlyness – You're a girl. Be proud of all that means. You are soft, you are gentle, you are woman. Don't try to be a guy. Guys like you because you are different from them. So let your girlyness soar.

2. Tell It Like It Is – *Dateable* girls don't lie to themselves. They don't say stuff like, "His girlfriend just isn't good to him—that's why he's seeing me on the side," or "She started it, so I'm going to get even." The *Dateable* girl lets God run the world and tells herself the truth, that all she can control is herself. She doesn't imagine things to be more than they are.

3. The Sexiest Thing on a Girl Is Happiness – Girls try so hard to add beauty and sexuality to themselves with clothes and makeup, but the truth is it's your spirit that makes you hot. Your outlook on life, your happiness factor. *Dateable* girls aren't downers. They love life.

4. Girls Don't Fight Other Girls—Ever – Revenge belongs to God. *Dateable* girls know that when they fight other girls, they look stupid and catty, and guys don't like it any more than God does.

5. Believe in Your Beauty – *Dateable* girls learn how to overcome the stuff people did to them in the past. They don't let the enemy steal their beauty. God made them, so they know they are beautiful, even if they don't feel like it sometimes.

6. Be Mysterious – *Dateable* girls know how to shut up. They don't monopolize the conversation. They don't tell everyone everything about themselves. They save some for later. They listen more than they gab.

7. Act Confident – *Dateable* girls know that confidence is hot. And the cool part is that no one knows if you are confident but you. Confidence isn't how you feel; it's how you act. Act confident and people will think you are.

8. Look 'Em in the Eye – Part of being a *Dateable* girl is really seeing people. People matter, but if you don't look them in the eye, then you will never really see them, and they will never know they matter to you. Look 'em in the eye because they are valuable.

9. Let Him Lead – God made guys to be leaders. *Dateable* girls get that and let him do guy things like get the door and open the ketchup bottle. They relax and let guys be guys. Which means they don't ask him out!

10. Need Him – *Dateable* girls know that guys need to be needed. A *Dateable* girl isn't Miss Independent. She knows we are made for community. Needing each other is part of faith. She allows him to be needed at times, knowing he was called to serve just as much as she was.

warning Never ask a guy what he's thinking. Chances are it isn't what you want it to be.

TRUE LOVE

RULES

Is It Real?

7 Q's to ask yourself to find out if it's true love:

1. What do I want from this relationship?

2. Does the other person want the same thing?

3. Am I feeling pressured in any way?

4. Am I better because of him/her in my life?

5. Do we both still have our own friends?

6. Do I feel guilty? Do I feel good about the physical stuff we do?

7. Do my friends and family approve?

The correct answers for love are: 1 = If you answered anything selfish here, then you might not know what love is all about, 2 = yes, 3 = no, 4 = yes, 5 = yes, 6 = no, 7 = yes

BREAK OUT THE DICTIONARY

DEFINING TRUE LOVE

Love is a decision, not a feeling. If it were a feeling, it couldn't be commanded by God. That's right, God can't command you to feel love any more than he can command you to feel giddy. Yet all over the Bible God commands us to love—to love him, our neighbors, even our enemies. Love is the action, not the feeling. Emotions are not commandable. But love is. True love is a decision first. Feelings may follow, but they may not. Either way, love never gives up.

God is the perfect example of love: "God so loved the world that he **gave** his one and only Son" (John 3:16). God's love is proven time and again in his giving, and so is true love between 2 people. It's all about the giving, not the receiving.

When 2 people truly love, they aren't connected at the hip and unable to function apart from the other. Both want what's best for the other one. Even in the middle of a fight, they still love each other. In other words, if you love, you care enough to give the person what they need, not what you need.

True love doesn't distract you from your purpose and vision; it focuses you better.

True love knows that you would be friends even if you weren't in love.

In true love both are givers; the relationship doesn't have one giver and one receiver.

In true love both trust each other.

In true love both are okay with the fact that the other one isn't perfect.

The Definition of Puppy Love

Puppy love is about how someone makes you feel.

Puppy love needs the other person in order to feel happy.

Puppy love means one person takes while the other one only gives.

Puppy love is jealous a lot.

Puppy love is draining, not energizing.

Puppy love is terrified that the other person will leave you.

Puppy love is obsessed with the other person.

definition **crush:**
an intense but usually short-lived infatuation

The Dirt Is Done

Well, the end is here, my dear. You've made it through the entire *Dirt on Dating*. Wow, another book on your "books I've read" list! How impressive! Definitely something to tell your friends about. And with your newfound knowledge, you can wow them with insight on the opposite sex. Stuff like the essentials of flirting and how to know if they "like you, like you." And if your list of friends just isn't enough, you can find even more people to chat with about dating stuff at www.ifuse.com.

On a more personal note, I really want to encourage you to spend some time thinking about *who you want to be* and *who you want to date*, or if you even want to date. If you desperately want to date but just aren't finding the right person, take courage, someday you will find someone to love you forever. In the meantime, spend your energy becoming someone that can *love another* forever. Spend time with God. Rest in the knowledge that he's got it all figured out and that the love of your life will come one day. Yes, maybe not soon, but one day you *will* find someone to love.

Hayley DiMarco writes cutting-edge and best-selling books including *Mean Girls: Facing Your Beauty Turned Beast, Marriable: Taking the Desperate Out of Dating, Dateable: Are You? Are They?, The Dateable Rules,* and *The Dirt on Breaking Up.* Her goal is to give practical answers for life's problems and encourage girls to form stronger spiritual lives. From traveling the world with a French theater troupe to working for a little shoe company called Nike, Hayley has seen a lot of life and decided to make a difference in her world. Hayley is Chief Creative Officer and founder of Hungry Planet, an independent publishing imprint and communications company that feeds the world's appetite for truth. Hungry Planet helps organizations understand and reach the multitasking mind-set, while Hungry Planet books tackle life's everyday issues with a distinctly modern spiritual voice.

cool author